## Praise for *The Soul Solution*

"*The Soul Solution* is the answer for women who want to have it all but are tired of how society has defined what 'all' really is. This book gives women permission to trust themselves, access their inner authority, and expand their lives beyond what they thought possible."

**Shefali Tsabary, PhD**
bestselling author of *A Radical Awakening*

"In this thought-provoking, witty, wise, and warm book, Vanessa invites readers to resist the pressure to do it all and start redefining success on their terms. This is a must-read for any woman looking to have a more fulfilling, creative, and joyful life."

**Gay Hendricks, PhD & Kathlyn Hendricks, PhD**
bestselling authors and transformational leaders

"*The Soul Solution* has a satisfying mix of psychology, spirituality, and practices. It offers invaluable tools for women who want to wake up to their true nature and find a stable source of happiness within. Highly recommended."

**Kristin Neff, PhD**
bestselling author of *Self-Compassion*

"Vanessa is to women and power what Brené Brown is to vulnerability."

**Andy Dunn**
author of *Burn Rate*, cofounder of Bonobos

"As someone who teaches and writes extensively about the soul and past lives, I can say from direct experience that Vanessa's wisdom and playful ability to help others find ways to connect with their soul will have a lasting impact."

**Ainslie MacLeod**
past-life psychic, bestselling author of *The Instruction*, and spiritual teacher

"*The Soul Solution* is like a PhD in mindfulness aimed at helping women of all levels to find their unique purpose. This is a book I will pick up again and again to use as a guide for my own growth and development."

**Anne Robie**
former Head of People at StubHub

"Vanessa Loder's book is an honest and enjoyable read about an issue that affects millions of women: exhaustion. If you are overwhelmed and frustrated, this book will make you feel seen and offer some practical, simple steps for saying goodbye to hustle culture."

**Celeste Headlee**
author of *Do Nothing*

"Vanessa has written an inspiring and courageous book for any woman who feels conflicted when what she thinks she 'should' want is not what her heart compels her to pursue. Reading this book is like having Vanessa constantly at your side—as a cheerleader, a fellow traveler, and a coach/thought partner. If you are a high-achieving professional woman who yearns for a more meaningful and fulfilling life regardless of the success you have achieved, *The Soul Solution* is for you."

**Carole Robin, PhD**
coauthor of *Connect*, former director of the Arbuckle Leadership
Fellows program at the Stanford Graduate School of Business

# THE
# SOUL
# SOLUTION

# THE
# SOUL
# SOLUTION

A Guide for Brilliant, Overwhelmed Women
to Quiet the Noise, Find Their Superpower,
and Feel Satisfied
*finally*

## VANESSA LODER

**sounds true**
BOULDER, COLORADO

Sounds True
Boulder, CO 80306

Published 2022

Book design by Meredith Jarrett
Illustrations © 2022 Meredith Jarrett

The wood used to produce this book is from
Forest Stewardship Council (FSC) certified
forests, recycled materials, or controlled wood.

Printed in Canada

BK06428

Library of Congress Cataloging-in-Publication Data

Names: Loder, Vanessa, author.
Title: The soul solution : a guide for brilliant, overwhelmed women to quiet the noise,
    find their superpower, and (finally) feel satisfied / Vanessa Loder.
Description: Boulder, CO : Sounds True, 2022. | Includes bibliographical references.
Identifiers: LCCN 2021061194 (print) | LCCN 2021061195 (ebook) | ISBN
    9781683649298 (hardcover) | ISBN 9781683649304 (ebook)
Subjects: LCSH: Self-realization in women. | Soul. | Intuition. | Change (Psychology)
Classification: LCC HQ1206 .L63 2022 (print) | LCC HQ1206 (ebook) | DDC
    155.3/3382–dc23/eng/20220110
LC record available at https://lccn.loc.gov/2021061194
LC ebook record available at https://lccn.loc.gov/2021061195

10 9 8 7 6 5 4 3 2 1

**For Eva and James.** May you know the light and love that you are and that's available to you, always.

**This book is dedicated to women everywhere.** May you feel inspired, uplifted, and empowered to realize your dreams, claim your rightful place in the big story, and together cocreate a world that is more soul based.

**To the readers of this book:** I hope all your dreams come true and your nightmares turn into doorways. I hope you know that I've got your back (so does the universe), and I'm holding your heart with tenderness as you move forward on your unique path. My dearest wish is that this book acts as a portal, a gateway, to your own deeper awakening, whatever that looks like for you. I hope you find your truth, your soul's voice, and you live it fiercely. I hope that together, as we each find our voice and access The Soul Solution, we can rewrite the script and change the world so it more closely resembles our beautiful dreams. And no matter what, I hope that you feel loved, seen, understood, and held as you read these pages.

# CONTENTS

## Disclaimer

While I have tried to include diverse stories, I also acknowledge this book in no way represents the entirety and diversity of human experiences. I've chosen to use the pronoun *she* and refer to women as the intended reader, to which I mean anyone who identifies as female (regardless of the gender you were born into). I hope you can receive the messages and lessons in this book without the specific language or examples getting in the way of you allowing whatever is in your highest good.

My intention is to be as inclusive and loving as possible. As a white, privileged woman, my experience is limited. I acknowledge this truth and am committed to examining my unconscious biases and continually expanding my awareness of the diversity of human experiences. Every life is equally valuable and sacred. Your individual heart and stories matter. They matter. And I honor them. I have also found that many universal truths of the soul transcend our individual experiences. I hope you can focus on these universal truths regardless of the specific details presented. Take what serves you and leave the rest.

# INTRODUCTION

She has achieved everything she set out to do, but
it has come at great sacrifice to her soul.

MAUREEN MURDOCK
*The Heroine's Journey*

I met Caroline when she was on the brink of collapse. Most days, her calendar was packed with nonstop meetings. During lunch, she would inhale a quick salad, rush through her parenting to-do list (e.g., sign up her kids for classes or respond to teachers), and power through emails before returning to meetings. Caroline loved many aspects of her demanding job, but it was taking a toll on her well-being. At home in the evenings, preparing dinner or playing with her daughters, Caroline's mood was tinged with bone-deep exhaustion. What she really wanted was to curl up in a ball and take a nap for three days straight. But she was too stressed to sleep. Her therapist and husband were worried: Caroline had recently developed severe migraine headaches that knocked her out for days at a time. She knew deep down that this frenetic lifestyle was not sustainable, but she couldn't seem to get off the hamster wheel. Having grown up in an unstable environment with a mother who was emotionally unavailable, Caroline craved financial security and was used to being supercompetent. But her driven, overachiever tendencies were taking a toll.

Then her father died.

At work, it was the end of a tough month in which Caroline had been toiling tirelessly to land an important new client for the firm, only to have that client go elsewhere. At her father's funeral, Caroline's mind was riddled with thoughts of her incomplete "to-dos" and all of the "shoulds" she had prioritized over what really mattered—her family and her dreams. Just as she was reflecting on these trade-offs, her eight-year-old daughter leaned across the pew. "Mommy," she said, "are you sad about work again?" It was the push Caroline needed to change.

If that wasn't enough, at the urging of a friend, Caroline joined my thirty-day meditation challenge for ambitious, overwhelmed women, which helped her begin a daily five-minute meditation and journaling practice. She was amazed at how time seemed to stretch like molasses when she was in that relaxed state, so different from her usual scarcity mindset in which she was constantly rushing around with never enough time.

"If you were to tune in to your heart and your intuition rather than your ego, mind, or wallet, what would your heart tell you it needs right now?" I asked her.

Caroline told me that for years she had dreamed of selling their small condo in San Francisco, moving to Oregon, and learning to garden. She had written this off as an unrealistic fantasy, but then she had a serendipitous encounter with a woman in a coffee shop who was selling her property in Oregon. It felt like Caroline's soul was calling her there. Looking at pictures of this woman's house, Caroline spontaneously burst into tears, goose bumps rising on her arms. A little voice in her head whispered, *That's your house.* It felt irrational, but also right.

Prior to working with me, Caroline would have dismissed her instincts. But now she was trying a radically new approach: I had taught her to pay attention to her emotional cues, soul whispers (that inner voice she heard), and energetic bread crumbs (those moments she felt energized and alive). Caroline got clarity on what was important to her and confided in her husband that she really wanted to make this change. It wasn't always easy; there were some tough conversations and trade-offs with her husband's job and proximity to family. But in the end, they agreed to put an offer on the house. Less than two months later, she was shocked to be living in her dream home. Caroline had always been taught that she had to grind for rewards. But when it came to realizing her wildest dreams, she was surprised that when she prioritized her truth and changed her mindset, things came with greater ease than expected.

It raised a fundamental question: What if the point in life isn't to "crush it" but to savor it?

2

For many women, chasing success doesn't just include constant hustling for the corner office, working on weekends, endless video conferencing, forsaking others to get to the top, or adopting a masculine persona (acting "tough" to make it in male-dominated industries). There's pressure to succeed in all aspects of our lives: to be the ideal worker, the perfect mother, and the supportive spouse and friend all at once. The result? According to a 2016 study published in the journal *Brain and Behavior*, women are twice as likely to suffer from severe stress and anxiety as men, and according to the United Nations, women globally spend about three times as many hours on unpaid domestic and care work as men on an average day (4.2 hours compared to 1.7).[1] These arrangements are not paying off. While women outnumber men in college and account for 51.4 percent of middle managers in the US, only 18 percent of the highest-level leaders and 8.2 percent of Fortune 500 CEOs are female.[2] Other factors, such as COVID-19, have only compounded this issue, as women disproportionately shouldered the extra caregiving and homeschooling responsibilities.[3]

We live in a fast-paced, always-on culture that prizes busyness. Advances in technology, enabling 24/7 connectivity, have shifted expectations and blurred the boundaries between work and home. We wake up feeling "behind" before our day has begun. When we aren't working, we listen to podcasts and obsessively try to maximize every minute, but to what end? We're too busy rushing around and optimizing our productivity to pause long enough to deal with this frenzied insanity. Most people live in a state of sympathetic nervous system overdrive, steeped in adrenaline-fueled fight or flight, focused only on knocking items off an endless to-do list. Amid these competing demands, women, conditioned to be people-pleasers and rule-followers, are overwhelmed, dissatisfied, and on the brink of collapse. Many can't even imagine a life that supports their ambition *and* their emotional well-being.

That's where I come in.

If you had told me fifteen years ago that I would be writing a book with *soul* in the title, I'd have thought you were crazy. But that was before I realized that there are two realities: one governed by our ego and one by our True Self. Our ego, fueled by external norms and expectations, is made up of various internal voices, personas, stories, beliefs, and "shoulds." The True Self is connected to the soul. While our ego is loud and insistent, our soul brings deeper wisdom. It's the part of us that knows we don't want to be a lawyer anymore, that this marriage feels lonely, or that we need more laughter in our life. Our soul holds our Truth with a capital *T*, and though we work to repress it, our Truth has a way of surfacing whether it's convenient or not.

In my twenties and early thirties, I thought the point of my career was to find "success" by working hard, earning money, striving for promotions, and continually learning (that last part still holds true). My ego guided my choices, behaviors, and beliefs, which, from an outside perspective, appeared to work well. Here is how my ego would describe my past to impress you: I graduated top of my class from Columbia University, and I took a high-paying investment banking job on Wall Street followed by a job with a prestigious private equity firm. I moved to California to get my MBA from Stanford and climbed the career ladder in Silicon Valley. I married a wonderful man and was on track to become a partner at my firm. On paper, I was crushing it. But I couldn't shake the nagging feeling that I was meant for more—more fulfillment, more purpose, more happiness. My traditional success wasn't bringing the satisfaction I'd been promised by our mainstream culture, which confused the heck out of me. For years, I had been following the rules, dotting all my i's and crossing all my t's.

What if the playbook itself is flawed?

I began to wonder if there was a better way to live. Could I be driven and productive without rushing, anxiety-fueled, through my days? Could I realize my dreams instead of satisfying everyone else's perceived expectations? Why was I constantly meeting other people's needs but ignoring my own, only to wind up feeling resentful and exhausted? How could I balance work, family, health, and hobbies? How could I honor my ambition *and* nourish my soul? I had been so busy following this prescribed path that I had no idea how to forge my own way forward. What the heck did I want to do with my "one wild and precious life"?[4]

What I had yet to realize was that by asking these questions, I had already started on the path to recognizing and listening to my soul.

Seeking answers like any good overachiever, I began researching, asking experts, and tapping into my friends' networks (from executive coaches to psychics). I read dozens of books, attended mindfulness and neuroscience training and silent meditation retreats. I basically got my PhD in soul-searching! Some things worked better than others. But gently, and sometimes not so gently, that accrued knowledge began to nudge me in a more authentic direction.

After many sleepless nights, I decided to stop playing by the rules laid out by society, and I quit my job to follow my heart and intuition instead. What happened next shook me to the core: my inner overachiever felt lost without someone else setting the gold standard.

I felt my soul calling me to something bigger, more meaningful, but I had no idea how to connect with or trust this inner wisdom.

There was no road map that I was aware of. So, over the last decade, I have dedicated myself to learning how to live a life of joy and success—on my own terms.

And that's how *The Soul Solution* was born.

If striving, people-pleasing, and pursuing achievement for achievement's sake has left you exhausted and unfulfilled, this book is for you. If you're at a crossroads, your priorities have shifted, and you're not sure what's next, you're in the right place. If you want more out of life but are unsure how to get it, welcome. *The Soul Solution* is designed to help you unpack the stories you've been told and uncover who you really are, so you can build a life you love and (finally!) feel satisfied.

Maybe you picked up this book because you are being called to something greater in your life. Perhaps you've heard me speak about mindful leadership at your company or at a conference or you watched my TEDx talk, "How to Lean In Without Burning Out," and you want to go deeper into these tools and practices. Perhaps you've compromised or given so much of yourself to others that you need to reclaim your wholeness. Maybe you've been a rule-follower, only to find yourself unrewarded. You've tried your darndest to be good enough—the perfect employee, spouse, mother, sister, daughter, friend—but you've hit a wall and lost yourself.

Good news! *The Soul Solution* is full of answers to help you access your deeper desires and potential. Well, actually, *you* are full of answers. You've just been so busy fulfilling other people's expectations that you've forgotten how to access your own truth. As someone who has experienced this transition, I am honored to offer you the tools you may need to come out the other side. You hold in your hands a road map back to *you*, one you can return to again and again.

There's no telling where your journey might take you, but it will make you feel more alive, clear, confident, and attuned, poised to share your unique gifts with the world. *The Soul Solution* is about saying *yes* to feeling good more often, expanding in creativity, love, ease, and abundance every single day.

## What Is *The Soul Solution?*

At its core, *The Soul Solution* is about helping you learn to hear, trust, and act on your innate wisdom, heart, intuition, and deeper truth rather than doing what you "should" do. Your instincts are strong, and while you may need to excavate your inner voice in order to hear it, it's there.

If you don't know how to do this or aren't sure if it's even possible, relax, you're already doing it. Your higher self guided you here with me right now. Trust her. She knows the way.

For most of our lives, we live with tunnel vision. We're so focused on getting through the day that we forget to ask ourselves if we're on the track we want to be on. Here's what I've learned actually matters: self-realization and connection to your inner power source rather than chasing approval or external power over others. The only Gold Standard that matters in the end is the one that comes from your soul.

At its heart, this journey is about you coming home to yourself. **What most women who come to me are really asking is, "Can I trust myself?"** In a culture that has invalidated and devalued innate feminine wisdom and feminine traits in favor of patriarchal values such as rational, linear, logical thinking above all else, this is a valid and understandable concern. In learning how to trust *your* inner guidance, you will discover a new way of being in the world that is empowering and life-enhancing. This is *The Soul Solution*.

## Why Do We Need *The Soul Solution?*

Women today carry a crippling burden of expectations and unconscious messaging about our value, duties, and roles in a patriarchal society.

Women have been so relieved to have a seat at the table that we haven't questioned how the table is set!

When we reconnect with our souls and empower ourselves to create, build, lead, and speak our truth, we will craft the radical, holistic solutions that our world needs. It is by each connecting with our true essence (our soul) that women will reclaim an unshakable sense of worthiness and a belief that "I deserve more, I deserve better, and I have the power to create it."

These changes—negotiating a four-day workweek without a salary cut for more family time, delegating chores to make time for passions and hobbies— may feel scary at first. The current system of power and privilege can only shift if we begin trusting and prioritizing ourselves—our souls.

## How to Get the Most Out of This Book

Change is 20 percent insight and 80 percent action. You can read books about swimming or mindfulness all day long, but it's when you jump in the pool or sit still on a meditation cushion that you reap the benefits. So, to help you embody these strategies and concepts, I've included **Flip the Switch** tools at the end of each chapter, as well as additional exercises called **Quick Soul Tips** throughout the book. These tools, journaling prompts, and activities are designed to help you implement *The Soul Solution* in micro moments throughout your day.

Give yourself permission to skip around and apply these tools in the best ways for you. Think of this like a carefully crafted research study you are conducting on yourself. You will try all these new strategies, notice your responses and reactions, observe how you *feel*, and then make your next set of choices.

No matter what, I hope you can sense how much I am with you every step of the way. I've got your back. (And so does the universe!)

### Getting Started

I recommend using a special, dedicated Soul Solution Journal for the exercises in this book in order to track your progress. Choose a notebook that brings you joy and just *feels* right! Trust yourself and your inner impulses. If you can't find a notebook, take notes on your phone, tablet, or computer, or just grab any old piece of paper.

## Intention Setting

One of the skills *The Soul Solution* will instill in you is to set a clear intention before beginning any new endeavor. An intention is a statement of desire. When you set one, you activate a part of your own receptivity and clarify direction.

For example, when I drive somewhere, I set the intention to arrive safely and on time. Sometimes I amplify the intention by visualizing my car pulling into our garage intact or traffic parting to let me through. As I pad down the wooden hallway at the end of a workday to play with our kids, I often set the intention to embody a loving presence while I'm with them.

My primary intention with this book is to connect with those who are seeking these teachings at this time—to cocreate with those who are asking to remember their connection to their soul, to discover and unleash their real power so they can have the impact they long to have in the world.

## Your Intention

To begin, set an intention to get clear on what you would like to receive from this book. Take a moment to sit with these questions: What would you like? Why are you here?

Some sample intentions:

I want to gain clarity on my next steps with ease and grace.

I would like to feel more calm and joyful on a daily basis.

I want to improve my relationship with myself, be kinder to myself, get my needs met, and have the impact I long to have.

Write down your intention in your Soul Solution Journal. This simple act will make you more likely to create it.

**I'm so happy you've made the decision to put yourself first.** When you make the decision to connect with your soul, you'll discover and unleash your true power. It will impact not only your life but also the world around you.

This book condenses ten years of soul searching
into an easy-to-follow format that you can apply to
your life immediately. Are you ready to begin?!

## Soul Symbols

This book came to me in a dream several years ago. During a 2 a.m. meditation, I had an intuition that I would be given symbols to include in the book that would change the vibration or energetic signature of the book itself. It seemed weird, but this whole book is about following our weirdness, so I trusted the guidance. The week before I was to turn in the final manuscript to my editor, I received *The Mayan Oracle* in the mail. When I looked at the cover and saw the symbol on the following page, my heart leapt and a quiet little voice inside whispered, *These are your symbols.*

Each chapter includes a symbol inspired by *The Mayan Oracle* for you to use as a focal point, or *drishti*.[5] Drishti is a Sanskrit word that means "view," "gaze," or "point of focus." It is a specific point on which to lock your eyes or inner vision during meditation or yoga. As you gaze at these symbols and repeat the accompanying affirmations, it will help you further integrate the deeper knowings and callings of your soul. If you feel inspired, you can draw one of the symbols on a sticky note and place it somewhere you will see it often. Notice how you feel in your body as you gaze at it. You can even draw one of the symbols on a key point on your body, like the inside of your wrist. Heck, go crazy, get a tattoo if you want. Tell everyone your soul made you do it. Your weirdness is welcome here, always.

## Soul Symbol

### CIB
(pronounced keeb)

This symbol represents trusting your inner voice of knowing and intuition. Breathe in and out deeply while gazing at this symbol and ask yourself, *What is the truth my heart wants me to know right now?*

I open to my inner truth with ease.

I say yes to receiving the inner guidance I seek.

*Chapter 1*

# BUT I FOLLOWED
# THE RULES

I grew up in the '80s and '90s, when second-wave feminism told me I could do anything, be anything, and compete with the best of 'em (a.k.a. boys). So I did.

I won math quizzes and got picked first in dodgeball; I was proud of my straight As, and skinned knees. In college, I played Division 1 soccer and graduated summa cum laude. On Wall Street, I cursed like a sailor, dressed in sharp blazers, and once wolfed down a seven-inch sub sandwich in under seven minutes on a dare while the senior partners cheered me on. Pulling all-nighters and working one-hundred-hour weeks was normal and something to brag about. It was a work-hard, play-hard culture in which I excelled, if I ignored the blatant sexism. As an eager new investment banking analyst, I beamed when a coworker said one of the managing directors had mentioned my name—until I found out it was while he perused company photos, listing who he wanted to have sex with.

That day, I muzzled my shock, revulsion, disillusionment, and sadness, but something in me began to crack. In subtle and not-so-subtle ways, I was being told where my value lay. Still, I put my head down, believing I could prove my worth through more prestigious jobs, business school, and more.

While I appeared successful on the surface, inside I felt anxious and unfulfilled. I would lie in bed at night with my mind racing with all the things I needed to do. Ever had that experience? Sure, everything in my life seemed "on track," but whose "track" was I really on? I had followed all the rules of the game, and yet I felt lost.

Women, particularly in the West, are reaching record levels of burnout from climbing the ladder only to realize the system is rigged and a glass ceiling remains. Women's chances of advancing are limited by sexism, conscious and unconscious bias, and microaggressions, no matter how hard we push ourselves.

And the cherry that topples the cake of exhaustion? Just as many women reach middle management, they're also starting families. The "mental load" of emotional and invisible labor, coupled with outdated gender norms, leaves women with an outsized share of the housework and caregiving burden. In fact, according to the *2019 Women in the Workplace* study conducted by McKinsey & Company and LeanIn.Org, 39 percent of women in dual-career relationships report doing most or all of the housework, compared to just 11 percent of men. And as employees become more senior, the disparity between women and men grows: 72 percent of senior-level women have a partner who also works, compared to only 37 percent of men.[1] Ambitious women are suffering from burnout at astounding rates. We've been following the rules, "leaning in," giving our all at work and at home, and it's killing us.

So, even if the traditional, ego-driven, myopic version of success is achievable, it comes at the cost of joy, harmony, fulfillment, and authenticity. Women can either opt out of this insanity or exhaust themselves trying to fit a square peg into a round hole.

Women (and men!) want more, but we want a different kind of more. We want to fulfill our true potential and have a meaningful impact with our work without sacrificing our sanity in the process. The Dalai Lama famously said, "The world will be saved by the Western woman."[2] What if, in order to save the world, we must first save ourselves from the insanity the world has become? We must stop listening to external voices and tune in to our inner authority instead. We must stop following their rules.

> But how can we quit the hustle without
> abandoning our audacious dreams?

As I learned during my awakening, the first stage of any journey of personal transformation is **awareness**.

Awareness usually begins with an acknowledgment of what you *don't* want and already know in your core:

Things are not okay.

This is not okay.

I am not okay.

Whether you're coming into honest awareness about your job, your marriage, your health, or a relationship, the process begins with acknowledging the scary, sometimes ugly truth that things are not how you would like them to be. There's a pain point that motivates you to look for answers. Though some of us are jolted awake by a sudden tragedy or crisis, for many women, awareness starts as a slow tug or disquiet inside. There is an unexplainable feeling of dissatisfaction that you can't quite pinpoint, a knowing in your bones that you are meant for something more. This subtle feeling gains momentum until you feel compelled to take a small action, such as reading a book (like this one!) or having a random conversation that surfaces new ideas and invites expansion into your life. Recognizing this is what allows you to begin to go from ignoring the call to owning your true power and purpose.

Maybe you are at an inflection point—changing careers, moving cities, getting divorced, mourning a loss, grappling with illness. Your path used to feel good, but somehow it has become too small to hold all of you. You don't want to climb another rung of someone else's ladder. You want clarity. You want to wake up feeling excited about your life. Something inside of you is calling you to a bigger and more mysterious journey. Welcome, dear one. I am so glad you are here.

If you're reading *The Soul Solution*, it's because you are being called on some level to wake up. If you are feeling fearful or apprehensive, you're in good company. It's a normal part of the process. If one part of you is thinking, *What the heck is this lady talking about?!* and yet some deeper, wiser part is whispering, *Stay, listen,* you're right on track.

There's an expression: pain pushes until pleasure pulls. Often our pain is the necessary motivation we need to create change. This is worth celebrating, even if it sucks temporarily.

What is the pain or dissatisfaction that brought you here today? What if this pain is your soul's way of getting your full attention?

Deep breath. It's okay. This is a very necessary and important first step to create change and get you to where you want to be.

Often when you're called to something greater, that call does not arrive like a pretty embossed piece of stationary with fancy gold cursive writing, spritzed with rose water. Instead, it arrives like a tiny splinter in your fourth toe. It doesn't even have the dignity to lodge itself in your big toe. Nope, it comes in one of your smaller, lesser-valued toes. So you ignore it. It's annoying, but you can deal with it. Some of us will limp through the rest of our lives with a splinter in our toe. Most of us keep walking until it becomes red and irritated. Then maybe you begin to grumble and complain, but you still don't stop to do anything about it. It's just an annoying little splinter, after all.

Until it's not.

Eventually you literally cannot take another step. You are *forced* to stop and pay attention to it. Only it's not your foot. It's your unsatisfying career or the spark that's missing from your marriage or how much wine you've been drinking. This is how most of us come into awareness. It ain't pretty, but it gets us to stop and address what needs to change.

## How to Gain Awareness

Here are five signs that you're being called to wake up to your truth. As you move through this list, rather than berating yourself if you identify with any of these signs, see if you can do a happy dance that you are coming into more awareness about your current situation. Your awareness is the spark that will inspire you to create change.

### 1. The Body Never Lies

Physical symptoms often denote a psychological or emotional conflict. If you're experiencing chronic pain, migraines, hypertension, repeated illness, or insomnia, it can be a sign that you're not living in alignment with your True Self. (If you're having trouble sleeping, use the Deep Sleep Guided Relaxation at vanessaloder.com/book.)

Also, start to notice anytime your body feels constricted, tense, or heavy. When you are out of alignment, you could have a tightness in your chest, a pit in your stomach, or a heaviness in your shoulders. The body never lies.

### 2. Mental Spinning

If you often find yourself in your head, confused, arguing with yourself, or trying to talk yourself into something, it may be because you don't feel good about what you have to do! Being stuck overanalyzing and feeling paralyzed can be a sign of misalignment with your deeper truth. Regardless of whether you truly want to be doing that thing or not, the mental spinning doesn't get you closer to your desires.

When I'm struggling to make a decision, it's usually because the answer is no and I'm scared to admit it. Even with minor situations (i.e., *Should I take the kids on a road trip to visit my sister this weekend?*), if I'm waffling it's usually because I don't really want to do it or I *do* want to but the timing isn't good.

### 3. Burnout

When you hit a wall of exhaustion and overwhelm, you're being called to make a change. You can try to push through and blame others (or yourself!), or you can pause and get curious. What is most out of balance right now? Almost every woman I know has suffered from burnout at some point, in part because we're culturally conditioned to take care of others and ignore our own needs.

## Quick Soul Tip

Burnout caveat—don't beat yourself up! It is vital for our self-worth and sanity as women to understand that if we feel exhaustion, it's often a result of current social, political, and cultural circumstances. Our patriarchal culture sets up unattainable beauty, success, romance, and parenting ideals. We've been taught to give, give, give without receiving from others or nourishing ourselves. Naming our present reality is not about blaming others or setting up a victim/villain dynamic but coming into a higher level of awareness. Many supposed "self-help" books shame women, inferring that overwhelm is solely our problem to fix. You are not broken! There are major systemic issues at play. If you are marginalized, the systemic issues loom even larger. Acknowledge this truth and then ask yourself, *What do I need to feel better?*

## 4. Procrastination

You feel unmotivated and unproductive. Don't worry! You're not lazy. You just may not *really* want to be doing that thing. Maybe you want to find work you're more passionate about, or caregiving is a higher priority for the time being. Either way, your lack of motivation comes from either being dishonest with yourself about what you *really* want to be doing with your time or feeling unsure of how to get there.

I used to think something was fundamentally wrong with me because I wasn't excited to sit in front of a computer for eight hours a day. Now I think there is something fundamentally off balance with our society because we treat human beings like machines and expect people to sit still in front of screens all day long.

## 5. The Hungry Ghost (Something Is Missing)

The hungry ghost, a Buddhist concept, is a being driven by animalistic need. Today, the term refers to the constant craving for more, more, more. It's an empty hole inside you that can't be filled no matter how much material wealth, accolades, or approval you accumulate. Your accomplishments don't fill the deeper ache within you (which is your soul urging you to wake up).

If you're experiencing one or more of the symptoms above, you're being called to look at truths that are perhaps uncomfortable or scary.

When things break down, it's important to acknowledge our hurt. Then we get to choose: Do we want to be intentional about how we put our lives back together and awaken to our own greatness? Or do we want to push through and repress the difficulty, clinging to old hopes and a false sense of stability?

Sometimes we're drowning and we don't even realize it. We need a loved one (or a stranger, or a book) to hold up a mirror.

I had this experience while suffering from postpartum difficulties (depression, hormone imbalance, identity loss) after my first child was born.[3] My good friend Jenny looked me in the eye and said, "Vanessa, you are *not* okay." That was the moment I realized I needed outside help. After addressing my hormone imbalances and adrenal fatigue and seeking therapy, I began to feel like myself again. Coming into awareness can make us feel vulnerable because we're admitting that we need help, yet vulnerability is the key to moving forward.

Now I want to ask you: Are you okay? Honestly—are you?

When we ignore the call to awareness, we feel discontented and frustrated. When we accept the invitation to step into our true potential, we feel clear, confident, and purposeful. Signs and serendipities may occur; things can start to feel natural and easy.

You now know how to find awareness as a seeker beginning the heroine's journey. Excited and nervous, you're on the cusp of something big.

# FLIP THE SWITCH

## Coming into Awareness
### How to Get to a 10

There's an expression in business: measure what matters. If you don't track important metrics, you won't improve upon them.

One of the most elegant tools I've found for measuring what matters when it comes to our overall well-being is inspired by Jack Canfield's book *The Success Principles*. Start by listing the areas of life that matter to you. For example: work, romantic relationship, family/friends, health, community, spirituality, hobbies. Choose four to eight categories. Then rank how satisfied you currently feel in each on a scale of 0–10. This exercise can be painful and eye-opening. You'll quickly grasp where you need to focus.[4]

If you notice yourself reverting to self-criticism about your low scores, try being kind and gentle with yourself instead. Remind yourself: *Taking an honest look at what's working and what's not is going to help me get more of what I want.*

Now here's the exciting and empowering part: Each day for the next week, ask yourself, *Which area of my life wants focus today?* Tune in to your heart and your intuition rather than your mind, allowing the answer to bubble up in your awareness.

Then, for whichever area you choose, ask, *How can I get this to a 10?* and come up with a simple action step you can take that day to move in that direction. (Research shows you are more likely to follow through on a goal if you write it down.[5]) Don't fret if you are at 2 or 3 and getting to 10 feels far away. Take baby steps. Going from 2 to 4 is a victory! Taking a small action step even once in the next week will initiate positive momentum to carry you forward on this journey.

For example: My low category to focus on today is giving back.

> **Action Step:** By 5 p.m. PST today, research volunteer opportunities in the Oakland/East Bay area, preferably mentoring inner-city kids or supporting disadvantaged women.

## Heart Wisdom and the Five-Foot Bubble

Here is a guided meditation script to help you tune in to your heart and ask some deeper questions. Even if you're new to meditation, just sit quietly and follow this script. If you would prefer to listen to this in audio format, go to vanessaloder.com/book.

If you have never meditated before, you can simply sit in a chair or cross-legged on the floor. Begin by sitting quietly and focusing on your breath. Place one or both hands on your heart. I like to visualize a little white light in the center of my heart and with each inhale that light gets bigger and brighter.

Call to mind an experience of gratitude or joy, perhaps with a child or an animal you love—an uncomplicated relationship. Expand this feeling of love in your heart and in your whole being.

Now that you are connected with your heart center, begin to float these questions into your awareness: *What do I want to cultivate more of in my life? What feeling do I want to experience more of today and this week?* By tuning in to your heart *first* as you bring this question to mind, you will receive a more soul-based and authentic answer.

Some potential values that may arise for you are: trust, satisfaction, joy, peace, balance, calm, and confidence. Notice what feels most alive and true for you today. Recently, for example, the word *satisfied* came up for me, with regard to growing both my marriage and business.

Next, visualize yourself surrounded in a bubble of this word. So, visualize "satisfied," for instance, five feet in front of you. (I like to gesture with my hands and make the sound *cha, cha, cha*.) "Satisfied" five feet behind you (*cha, cha, cha*). "Satisfied" five feet to your left and right (*cha, cha, cha*). "Satisfied" five feet above and below you (*cha, cha, cha*).

Now you're awash in this golden bubble of "satisfied" light. Imagine, envision, or sense yourself going about your day while remaining inside the bubble: Finishing a project at work (feeling satisfied)—what would that look like or feel like? Spending time with loved ones (feeling satisfied)—how will you act? What will you say or do? Completing a mundane task such as loading the dishwasher or wiping crumbs off the counter (feeling satisfied).

Lastly, visualize yourself lying in bed tonight, reflecting on your day while still surrounded by your bubble. You drift off to sleep feeling deeply *satisfied*.

## Soul Symbol

## The Ray of Dissonance

This symbol represents the process of disintegration that occurs when the rigid walls of old beliefs and constraints that "no longer serve your emerging wholeness" begin to crumble. "Anything that presently defines and limits you is being stripped away."[6] Breathe in and out deeply while gazing at this symbol and ask yourself, *What old structures or beliefs am I ready to surrender?*

I let go of what no longer feeds me with grace and ease.

I say yes to my True Self.

# Chapter 2

# THE WHISPERS
# OF YOUR SOUL

When you begin searching or asking deeper questions about your life, you may be surprised to discover that your soul is always present, signaling to you. Like most of us, you've just become really good at blocking it out. Here's why: **The soul speaks to us in whispers during little slivers of silence we create in our minds.** The ego, in contrast, shouts at us constantly. For many people, the voice of the soul isn't even something that's heard so much as felt or sensed. Others get "truth bumps," like goose bumps, up and down their arms and body when they're in the presence of truth. Sometimes there's just a knowing or gut feeling without rational explanation.

This isn't like a seventh grader's birthday party where only the cool kids get invited. We all get invitations (several!) to awaken. Many of us need several nudges and even a few solid whacks before we finally RSVP to our soul's invitation.

Once I started listening, one of the first places my soul led me was to a Holiday Inn ballroom in downtown San Francisco. On stage, Brian Weiss, an expert in past life regression hypnosis, was about to hypnotize the over two hundred attendees at once. The lights dimmed, psychedelic music started playing, and I thought, *Have I lost my mind? This is nuts!*

At the time, I considered myself a strategic thinker, not someone who trusted mystical forces for big life decisions. This was way out of my comfort zone. But during my search for answers, I'd been led to this moment by a series of books and bread crumbs. I couldn't ignore a deeper, quieter voice urging me on. While hypnotized, I had a direct experience of a past life that had a profound impact on me and my perception of what it means to be a soul incarnated in a human body.

I didn't know it at the time but that event would mark a pivotal moment in my life. Whether I realized it or not, my greater soul awakening had begun.

So, here's the good news: when you follow the quiet whispers of your soul, you end up somewhere magical, as opposed to letting your ego lead and winding up with only hollow projections of success. The ego's loud voice can order you to plant crops, but it can't lead you to a meadow of wonder, filled with wildflowers you didn't even know you loved or needed. When you realize those are the *exact* blooms you've been desperately craving all your life, you'll truly understand the importance of trusting your soul. And that's where we're headed.

## Core Self versus Autobiographical Self

The Portuguese American neuroscientist Antonio Damasio uses the terms *autobiographical self* and *core self* to describe what I am labeling as the *ego* and *soul* respectively. Women's leadership expert Tara Mohr interprets Damasio's term "autobiographical self" to consist of the stories we tell about ourselves or who we think we are: "I'm a good daughter," "I'm always on time," "I'm a vice president at a tech company," "I'm attractive (or unattractive)."[1]

The core self, in contrast, is the *experiencing* self. I interpret the core self to be the part of us that asks: *How do I feel right now, at this moment? What is my intuition saying? What do I know in my bones to be true?*

Most of us exist primarily as the autobiographical self, and this causes a lot of suffering and misalignment. Your core self might want to take a dance class or write a book, but your autobiographical self will say, *Dancing isn't a viable career, especially for you.* Your core self might feel blah when you spend too much time on social media. But your autobiographical self will respond, *You need to be on social media to stay current. Look at how much better everyone else is doing.*

If you only listen to your autobiographical self or ego, you're more likely to make choices that don't reflect who you really are or what truly makes you come alive. Instead, you want to begin more consistently connecting with your core self.

One clue that you're hearing your soul's voice is that your ego will proba-bly judge it, labeling your soul's voice as "weird," "stupid," "insignificant," or "impossible." Your soul whispers may appear to be nonstrategic, nonlinear, and irrational, and they may not jibe with who you think you're supposed to be. For example, I was an established private equity investor who found herself in a room full of strangers about to experience past lives. It doesn't get more dichotomous than that. In the beginning it rarely makes sense. If it seemed sensible, you'd already be doing it.

Some of you already know what your soul is calling you to do. You've just allowed fear—of failure, of not belonging, of your own greatness—to get in the way. Others are less sure and feel panicked or impatient about finding their purpose.

In truth, most people don't identify with having a single "soul calling," even though the overachiever in us wants to put it in a nice tidy box we can explain to the world.

Years ago, when I thought my calling was some singular, purpose-driven entity, I felt simultaneously inadequate and pressured to find it. Now, I've been following (sometimes chasing) my soul's calling for years and have dis-covered that there isn't just *one thing* I'm here to do. I have many higher purposes to explore in my life, and they evolve as I evolve.

Actually, your soul is calling you All. The. Time. In big and small ways. Your soul is there, just beneath the surface of your ego, calling you to live from a place of love rather than fear, to be grateful rather than grasping, to be in abundance rather than scarcity, and to live in alignment with your deepest desires.

So, think of your soul calling not as a singular thing but as an ongoing invitation.

Maybe your soul is calling you to go out in nature more often, to laugh more, to spend more time playing with your children instead of doing their laundry. These soul whispers can arrive as random impulses—to contact someone you haven't spoken to in years, to wear more yellow and less black, to take an art class, to read a random book, or to plant flowers in your garden. To stop taking yourself so seriously.

As you begin to recognize these "random impulses" as soul whispers, you will be less likely to dismiss, devalue, or abandon them. The more time you spend being still and quiet with yourself, the easier it becomes to tune in to this voice that can eventually lead you to something bigger, such as more creative or mission-driven work. But that's not the point for everyone. The point is to honor and act on all your small callings and let them lead you to a more fulfilled life.

## Connecting with Your Soul

Here are three steps to connecting with your soul and receiving its guidance:

### Step 1: Quiet the Ego

Think of your ego as a cranky toddler, sitting in the back seat of your car, whining constant questions and demands: *Are we there yet? I spilled my pretzels. Baby shark doo doo doo doo doo doo, baby shark! More pretzels! Oh look, a motorcycle. Look, look, LOOK!*

If you're a parent, you know how exhausting and distracting that incessant chatter can be. How the heck are you supposed to focus on the GPS with this voice piping up every three seconds? Next thing you know, you've spilled coffee in your lap, then taken the wrong exit off the freeway!

It's the same with our ego. It's nearly impossible to hear the quiet nudges of our soul when our ego is yelling at us that we're a loser, doomed to fail, or that we should choose law school over art school. (Our ego can sound very rational and adultlike—*Of* course *you should stay at your current job; other people would be thrilled to have your situation*—but it's still a toddler at heart.) It is not surprising that we take the wrong exit when our ego is bombarding us with negative messages! We can't think or feel straight.

Your mind will repeat itself over and over again if you leave it on autopilot. Approximately 90 percent of our daily thoughts are recurring:[2]

*I need to call Beth; her daughter's been having a hard time. Ugh, I haven't finished that work project. I need to eat more healthy food. I'm going to the gym tomorrow. I need to call Beth. I'm really going to focus and finish this work project. I hope Beth's okay. I'll definitely order a salad for lunch.*

And on and on it goes.

The only way to break this cycle is to interrupt its circuitous loop. Meditation is one of the simplest and most effective tools to interrupt your "monkey mind" (a Buddhist term for restless thoughts) and help tune your inner radio to a different station. Any quiet time, from baths to nature walks, can also help. It takes practice to witness, but as you observe these repetitive loops, you'll naturally calm the ego and create space for a new, more authentic voice to come through with the whispers of your soul.

## Step 2: Differentiate Ego versus Soul

The second step to following your soul whispers is to begin differentiating ego from soul. All you have to do is pay attention.

The ego pushes and pushes. No matter what you do, it's never enough. The ego is driven by the need to please and the desire to earn approval and accolades in order to feel safety and a sense of belonging. Many of us have internalized the voices of our parents or our culture without fully realizing it, so the ego seems to be logical and linear. Your mind—rather than your heart, body, or intuition—is driving the bus.

The soul, on the other hand, often originates outside of your rational mind and allows for expansion. When it comes *through* you, its message feels deeply true.

This is not about getting rid of the ego. It's about *integrating* it. It carries essential information about our growth and healing. If we look closely, the ego offers a gift, shining a light on our unresolved pain and trauma.

The problem emerges when we begin to see the ego's narrative as truth, often reinforced by our rigid broader culture. In reality, our planet and its leadership would look very different if people allowed their hearts and intuition to guide them. If we want lives aligned with our souls, we have to make a conscious effort to trust those quieter impulses even if they feel unorthodox. Finding a community that values and affirms those deeper impulses is a great way to get the support and courage we need on this path.

## Quick Soul Tip

Stand up (somewhere private where you won't be self-conscious) and imagine your ego is driving the bus, making you worried about what other people think, grasping, striving, shoulding, people-pleasing. Assume a posture that reflects your ego is in the driver's seat. For example, mine is standing with one hand on my hip, one arm outstretched with the pointer finger directing me forward in an aggressive manner, like a general at war. This elicits a feeling of control and rigidity.

Break out of this state: wiggle around or shake your hands to get back to neutral.

Next, imagine you are allowing your soul to guide you. Set a timer for one to three minutes. Move your body in whatever ways you feel inspired. Allow the impulses to come from within. Maybe you start off stretching, touching your toes, and then you feel an urge to wiggle from side to side. Suddenly you feel called to sway your hips. Simply go from movement to movement without judgment, allowing a deeper knowing to guide you. If you like, end this practice lying on the floor with arms and legs outstretched wide like a starfish. This can elicit a feeling of surrender and feeling supported.

### Step 3: Slow Down and Connect with Your Soul

It's important to slow down and get still to hear your soul because it doesn't speak in words. Your soul speaks in longings, feelings, symbolism, dreams, nature, and synchronicity.

Have you ever had a profound experience in nature? Perhaps you witnessed a gorgeous sunset that made you feel incredibly alive and then found that descriptive language didn't do it justice. That's your soul speaking directly to you.

You know your soul is speaking to you when:

- You notice signs and coincidences.

- You feel in flow, as though you're being guided by a larger force.

- You are deeply connected with your creativity.

- You sense in your gut that something is your truth.

- You judge your impulses as unusual or different.

- You sense a soul-level connection with someone else.

## Reclaim Your Wild Nature

Whether you can describe it or not, pausing to watch a sunset or engaging with nature in whatever way possible is one of the best ways to quiet your mind and connect with your soul. In the West, we're taught to live in our heads. Think of the last time you faced a dilemma: Did you do a lot of mental gymnastics trying to solve the problem? We have disconnected from our bodies and hearts, and from nature herself, from the cycling seasons and lunar phases to the energy that keeps the planets spinning. What if the answer to your dilemma could be inferred by a hummingbird appearing just as you have a certain thought? Or the right next step is revealed as you're sitting quietly under your favorite oak tree and are startled into realization by an acorn falling to the ground right at your feet? These "coincidences" may well not be accidental—you are now staying still and open enough to see them.

You don't need to live in a house in the mountains to access nature. Go to your favorite spot at your local park. Take a walk on the beach. Dance under the moon. Maybe there are benches under a tree outside of your local library or in the courtyard at a museum. Just take some time to be in your body and connect with the smells and sensations around you.

In *Soulcraft*, Bill Plotkin suggests dialoguing with nature by wandering aimlessly with a journal until something captures your attention—a tree, rock, furry critter, dew on a blade of grass, cloud, or any other aspect of nature. Sit quietly and observe, share your current dilemma or life story, ask a question, and notice how nature responds.[3] This isn't about nature answering a specific question (although that happens with astounding frequency). It's about reclaiming your true nature by being one with Mother Earth. It's a reminder of the wild and free you, which allows all the illusory problems to recede. When you spend this time in solitude, you remember the greatest wisdom can always be found at the heart of you and in connection with the broader web of life.

Ever the good student, Priya followed my advice to dialogue with nature and dutifully took her journal to a local reservoir. Afterward she recounted:

> *Vanessa, I felt so weird walking along the path, trying to choose a rock or tree to speak to. Plus, I was self-conscious that someone would hear me talking to a rock and think I was a crazy lady. But then, as I found a beautiful, secluded spot along the path and asked some deeper questions about my life (to a tree!), I saw a flock of white birds that reminded me of my mother, and something in my heart just clicked. All of a sudden, I had this random idea that I really need to take me nine-year-old son to India. There was just this knowing. I was scared to tell my husband about my vision. I had done the Heart Wisdom and the Five-Foot Bubble, and the word that emerged was* Brave. *And then as I was driving home from the reservoir, I saw the word* Brave *in GIANT letters on the side of a big barn!! So I decided to be brave. Funny enough, when I brought it up to my husband, he thought it was a great idea. And now the original impulse has expanded with another bread crumb to talk to my son's teacher about having a third-grade class in India be pen pals with my son's class in the United States. Eventually I want to take a group of kids to India on a service trip. All of this came from me talking to a tree.*

Nature heals and gives us answers to our most profound and longing questions. She restores us to ourselves, letting us hear our souls loud and clear.

# FLIP THE SWITCH

## Soul Speak Practices

Your soul responds to ceremony, even something as simple as lighting a candle and setting an intention. Let your heart and intuition guide you in choosing one or two of the below practices to experiment with in the next week. Allow it to be fun and easy, not another should.

You can begin by creating a sacred space for your ceremony. *Sacred Space* is just a fancy way of saying a special spot. It's an area in your home that feels safe, cozy, and downright lovely to you. You can create your sacred space by choosing a really luxurious or soft, worn blanket, or buying a candle that feels indulgent and brings you joy, and laying these objects out in a particular corner or nook of your home. Maybe your sacred space is in a room facing a pretty view, or includes your favorite, comfy chair.

> **Creativity:** Choose a creative endeavor such as writing, painting, sculpting, pottery, gardening, cooking, baking, singing, reading poetry, or dancing to put you more closely in touch with your soul.

> **Meditation + Ceremony:** Go to your sacred space and light a candle, set an intention, or make a prayer for guidance. Sit in silence and meditate: focus on your breath to create quiet space for your soul whispers to come through. One simple ceremony is to write on one piece of paper something you want to let go of, burn it, then write on another piece of paper what you want to invite in and keep that paper on your nightstand or somewhere special. Or follow your intuition and make up your own ceremony.

As one client shared, "I didn't realize I could create my own ceremony. I thought someone had to tell me what to do because I was raised in the church where there was a prescription. The other day, I got into a toxic conversation with my dad. Afterward, I walked to the beach and decided to do a ceremony for myself. I scooped up all this sand, spoke into the sand all my hurts and disappointments, and then let it go through my fingers while saying 'I'm releasing this and I'm wishing you well.' And I instantly felt better. There is empowerment that comes from recognizing you can create these types of ceremonies."

**Dialogue with Nature:** Go into nature and speak to it, aloud at first. Choose a tree, a rock, an animal, the sunset, or any other aspect of nature to dialogue with. Thank them for being there, ask them a question or talk to them about your situation or dilemma. See how they answer; it may be with a feeling or something they physically do (a chipmunk chatters, a tree drops a pinecone, etc.). Imagine you can understand what they want to tell you.

## Journaling Prompts

Answer these questions in your Soul Solution Journal:

Can you remember a time when you chose the voice of ego rather than soul? What happened? How did you feel?

Write about a time when you had a "knowing" about something. Did you listen? What happened?

What has most supported you in connecting with your soul voice?

## Soul versus Ego Quick Checklist

If you aren't sure whether ego or soul is in the driver's seat, scan this checklist and notice which feels most true:

| Ego | Soul |
| --- | --- |
| Pushes | Pulls |
| Loud voice, demanding | Gentle whisper, calling |
| Control | Surrender and grace |
| Pleasing others | Pleasing self |
| Hustle | Savor |
| Logical, realistic, strategic | Irrational, "crazy," nonstrategic |
| Predetermined plan | Emergent, meandering |
| Force | Flow |
| Effort | Ease |
| Confused | Clear |
| Unsatisfied | Fulfilled |
| Chasing external validation | Connected to inner values |
| Stagnant | Expansive creativity |
| Burned out | Energized |
| Advancement | Alignment |
| Unworthy | Intrinsically worthy |
| Fear | Love |

## Soul Symbol

## Muluc
(pronounced moo'-look)

This symbol represents self-remembrance. Begin noticing signs, serendipities, signals, symbols, and heightened perception coming to you and through you. Breathe in and out deeply while gazing at this symbol and say to yourself: *I open my third eye, the cosmic raindrop, to receive clear and direct access to the guidance I seek.*

I am open to my divine path.

I say yes to receiving clear and direct guidance from the universe.

*Chapter 3*

# YOUR ENERGETIC BREAD CRUMBS

When I followed my own soul whispers and left a high-paying, stable job to find work I loved, it was scary as hell. Initially I gave myself six months to follow my heart and intuition (though I had no idea how to do that). If things didn't work out, I figured I could always go back into finance. I felt like I was jumping off a cliff. But then something utterly unexpected happened.

Within a few weeks of quitting my job, several people approached me for advice because they wanted to quit *their* jobs. I was in the midst of completing a coaching certification, following what I call an "energetic bread crumb," but I wasn't necessarily planning on becoming an executive coach. Yet I would leave these coffee meetings feeling incredibly energized and alive. It felt good to share my story and offer strategies and resources. This led to a major aha moment that steered me toward executive coaching.

Learning to follow energetic bread crumbs is another key secret to unlocking The Soul Solution. Your energetic bread crumbs are the little nudges, good feelings, impulses, or experiences that excite you and bring you alive. Energetic bread crumbs offer clues to what makes you feel aligned with your True Self. They naturally guide you toward activities, people, places, and experiences that will bring you joy and lead to your most satisfying and meaningful life. I call them "bread crumbs" because, like Hansel and Gretel, you have to pay attention to notice them as they can be easily overlooked, but they *will* lead you out of the woods. They will lead you home—back home to your True Self.

Think of your energetic bread crumbs as little nuggets of joy you derive from encounters with others or tasks where you're in "flow" energy; when you're not overthinking, overanalyzing, or worrying about others' impressions of you and you're able to feel all the warm fuzzies inside.

As one friend described it,

> As an overachiever and "hustler," I'm constantly multitasking, planning, executing, and moving on to the next checklist item. These are undoubtedly important traits for running a house and managing a career, but energetic bread crumbs are where I derive true joy during the day and over longer periods of time. For example, I can be reviewing someone's work in a spreadsheet (yes, believe it or not, I love that feeling of understanding a formula in an Excel cell), discussing what I love about art with a teacher at my child's school, having a soulful one-on-one conversation with someone where we just click, or imagining a field day for my son's eighth birthday and envisioning the joy that capture the flag will bring to him.
>
> There is no one area where I derive these daily energetic bread crumbs, but they are nourishing and grounding for me and remind me that life doesn't always need to be lived in the hustle and the "should," and that I can slow down, listen to flow energy, and approach work and my family with more purpose. For me, there are underlying elements of creativity and belonging where I most often experience these energetic bread crumbs, and I continue to unpack that, listen to it, and pursue my intent of living more in the energetic-bread-crumb space than purely in the hustle space.

You may tend to dismiss your energetic bread crumbs as trivial because they're so natural to you. Yet what makes you feel alive is going to be different from what makes others feel alive. Kristen Wheeler, my dear friend and creator of the Native Genius® Method, says, "These small moments that light you up are easy to overlook yet key because they point to your innate gifts and your potential for success, fulfillment, and belonging." Your energetic bread crumbs are unique, and they are essential to finding your most soul-centric life. In the beginning, these situations can be subtle. The key is to keep following your bread crumbs to discover what energizes you. One small bread crumb leads to another, which leads to another. If you keep following them, your energetic bread crumbs will lead you to your soul's deepest longings.

This is about noticing what you naturally enjoy and then being intentional with your life and career. If you're engaged by a certain project at work, how can you design your career to do more of that type of project? If you enjoy connecting with someone in your community, what is it *specifically* about that person or conversing with them that enlivens you?

## Quick Soul Tip

Start to notice your energetic bread crumbs. When do you feel most energized and alive? After a meeting at work or a conversation with a friend, how do you *feel*? Which parts of the activity or interaction felt good to you? Don't overanalyze the "why," simply notice the bread crumbs.

Get curious: *What are my energetic bread crumbs telling me about the types of situations, people, and experiences that I want more of? How can I structure my day and life overall to have more of that?!*

As you seek The Soul Solution and shed aspects of your old identity, it's natural to feel untethered and confused. Don't worry: your energetic bread crumbs are both your sustenance and the lantern that will illuminate your path forward.

Your autobiographical self will demand to know, *Where is this all going?* The ego wants certainty and likes everything mapped out in advance. But your core self doesn't work that way. The soul reveals itself to us in increments. Allow yourself to be surprised by your energetic bread crumbs and follow them even if (especially if) they are not what you "should" do.

Steve Jobs, the cofounder of Apple Inc., once described this perfectly in a commencement speech when he said, "You can't connect the dots looking forward; you can only connect them looking backward. So you have to trust that the dots will somehow connect in your future. You have to trust in something—your gut, destiny, life, karma, whatever."[1]

Your energetic bread crumbs are not just about finding deep professional meaning. They are the moments when something inside of you goes *Ding ding ding! That's what I want to do! That's what makes me feel alive! That's what I'm interested in.* Your energetic bread crumbs are also the things that lead to the thing, that leads to the thing that makes you most aligned with your True Self.

## Energetic Bread Crumbs = Curiosity + Intuition + Feelings of Aliveness

My client Aubrey's twelve-year-old daughter, a budding dancer, told her parents she wanted to go to a different school focused on the performing arts. At first, Aubrey and her husband told their daughter to wait and apply when she is older. But then, as Aubrey reflected to me, "My daughter told me she can only make the next right decision, and I realized, oh wait, those are *her* energetic bread crumbs. We want her to hear herself and know she can act on her inner callings and desires and that we will support her in the process of becoming true to who she really is. She's naturally following her bread crumbs, and if I don't screw it up as her parent, she'll get there on her own."

At its essence, following your energetic bread crumbs is about being more loyal to you, to your higher self. Trusting that *only you* can know what you need. This process is also about trusting the mystery and your own divinity. As you take action based on this inner guidance, you'll be surprised by where it leads you. The challenge is to commit without guarantees about how things will work out. This is why so many of us struggle with this process. It makes us feel incredibly vulnerable.

I can promise you from direct experience, and from having supported hundreds of women in this process, that it always works. If you truly listen to and follow your energetic bread crumbs, they *will* lead you to greater happiness. It might take longer than you'd like. It might look different from what you would have predicted. But you will arrive at a more joyful and authentic destination.

Years ago, I worked with a client who was a senior leader at a nonprofit. She was tired of endless fundraising, but she still wanted to make the world a better place. She felt stuck. Following my advice to trust her intuition and follow her energetic bread crumbs, she signed up for a seemingly random video editing class and accepted an invitation to get coffee with a woman outside her industry. She had no strategic plan, but she described a "feeling" in her body telling her to say yes to this meeting. Three months later, that same woman introduced her to another woman who was hiring someone to help nonprofits tell their stories through video. My client was the perfect candidate for the job. She was in awe of how this unpredictable process worked.

My client couldn't have consciously identified her trajectory in the beginning. She didn't know exactly what she wanted. Yet the universe and her higher self were guiding her toward her own greatest fulfillment and highest good. Pretty cool, right?!

## Permission to Not Be "Ready"

If you are a rule-follower, accustomed to collecting gold stars, you may believe you need to be "qualified" or officially prepared before diving into something new. An internal report at Hewlett Packard showed that men apply for a job when they meet 60 percent of the qualifications, while women only apply if they meet 100 percent of them.[2]

Your reticence may not be a sign that you need more experience before trying something new. You may never feel completely ready or comfortable when you're stretching yourself. Don't get so focused on checking all the boxes that you forget to check the most important box of all: How do you *feel* when doing this? Does it energize you?

When you take action toward something that you're interested in, you also open yourself to more possibilities and create momentum. You may learn of a tangential class, field, or program that's an even better fit.

So, even if you give yourself a finite period of time, focus on following your energetic bread crumbs with a sense of curiosity, openness, and trust. You're not looking for immediate results or perfection. You're honoring the way each bread crumb will lead to another and another until you're standing on more solid ground.

Trust the process and let go of the
end result, at least for now.

If you are in a career transition, instead of obsessively updating your résumé, try dancing to good music to reach a high vibration (or energy state), then set a clear intention, such as "I want to find work that energizes and inspires me, uses my unique gifts and skills, and allows me to work in collaboration with thoughtful, happy people. I surrender, allow, and trust the universe to help me connect with the right people and next steps for my highest good at this time." Then reach out to people, not for "strategic net-working" (blah!) but because something about their background intrigues you or gives you a good gut feeling (yay!).

If you lapse into "compare despair" (*She got a new promotion; I'm behind!*), self-criticism (*I'm terrible at everything!*), or a shame spiral (*Why would anyone respond to my request?*), label these inner-critic voices, ground yourself in your intention, or take a break.

It's more important to feel good
than to take a specific action.

Or let's say you're single and looking for a joyful romantic partnership. If you join a dating app from a place of "shouldness" and notice that you're dreading creating your profile, don't do it. Instead, set a clear intention and then follow your energetic bread crumbs: "I commit to joyfully receiving a romantic partner who makes me laugh and helps me feel seen, adored, and supported." Maybe you get an impulse to buy a beautiful card and write yourself the love letter you would one day like to receive. If it brings you energy, trust the impulse and do it.

## Prioritize Downtime

Even an everyday act, such as going on a walk, can invite the bread crumbs you need. Perhaps as you're noticing all the ways that nature brings beauty and love into your life, suddenly an old friend's face flashes across your mind and gives you a warm, happy feeling. Reach out and see what happens next. Again, the key is to get quiet, be alert to any impulses, and then follow your energy, curiosity, and intuition to the right next step for you.

The good news is that you can start this process today. You can start small. Let's say you want to make a career change. Begin by listening to what you want to eat for breakfast or who you want to catch up with over coffee. It can have nothing to do with your career. It doesn't matter. It's the same voice guiding you and, as you listen to that guidance in one area of your life, it becomes easier to hear it overall. Just tune in.

If you can't hear that voice or don't sense any energetic bread crumbs, don't panic! Please don't judge yourself. You are not alone. Take a deep breath to allay your anxieties. Set the intention to tune in to your inner wisdom, then *forget* about your intention. Go do something that brings you joy. Eventually you'll notice a little nudge poke through. But if you put pressure on yourself, you might block your ability to receive. Don't force it. Take some time and space alone and simply notice what emerges.

I know that in our jam-packed, busy-as-a-badge-of-honor world, it's not easy to schedule downtime—and yet it's so important. If you're excited to learn more about a certain topic or hobby, take a class, read a book, or start a conversation with someone knowledgeable. Even if there's no logical reason—especially if there's no logical reason!—if you're curious about something and it brings you energy, do it.

Children are brilliant at following their energetic bread crumbs. If you have little people around you, watch how they flow from one desired activity to the next without assessing whether they're being productive. They simply follow impulses of joy.

If you're anything like me, it's extremely hard to schedule unscheduled time—even for downtime. The first time I intentionally allowed myself to *do nothing* except follow my desires in the moment, I felt extreme anxiety. I was scared that no impulses would arrive or I would do it "wrong." This experiment also highlighted how deeply ingrained my beliefs were that I wasn't valuable unless I was *doing* something.

All those energetic bread crumbs add up to a cake! These random, small acts eventually guide you to some bigger, more solid idea, project, relationship, or experience. They also guide you to an overall richer way of living. But you need to collect them, follow them, and allow them to nourish you. You do this by setting aside time each day to follow your impulses and your energy, not your shoulds. Try the following exercise.

## Quick Soul Tip

Each day, set a timer for ten to fifteen minutes and simply follow whatever impulses arise in that window. Tune in to your body and heart and do whatever brings you joy that day. There is no set plan for how to spend this time. Be surprised by what emerges. Maybe you are deeply exhausted and you want to lie on your back on the floor listening to soothing music. You might have an impulse to call someone, text someone, move something from here to there, or lie on the grass. Maybe you have an impulse to make yourself a cup of tea, then the cover of a particular book flashes through your mind. That means you have an impulse to read that book. So you do. Don't judge the impulses, just follow them. Notice how you feel before and afterward.

### Intentional Bread Crumb Time

Once a week, intentionally follow energetic bread crumbs related to a specific desire or important area in your life for an hour if you can. For a career transition, begin with a clear intention—for example, "I want to find work that energizes and inspires me. I intend to open my heart to receive guidance and clarity." Sit quietly until you receive an impulse or spend that time intentionally following up on previous bread crumbs. Sign up for an online art class, walk by the ocean, dig into the soil as you garden, or lie on the deck reading. Again, don't judge the impulses, honor them. After lounging around reading magazines, noticing your inner critic saying, *You are being lazy; this is a waste of time you could be using to organize the pantry*, and reminding yourself there are other wise voices inside, you may find that suddenly a new impulse arrives. You'll see an ad in a magazine that sparks an idea or find an online class that energizes you. That is your next bread crumb. And so on, and so on.

For the next two weeks, use the hour of "Intentional Bread Crumb Time" to take that online class or follow up on that spark of an idea.

There is no right way to do intentional bread
crumb time. What's important is to set aside **time
and space** to follow the nudges you receive.

## Focus on Energy, Not Output

To identify your bread crumbs, start to pay attention to your energy. When do you feel most alive, inspired, or curious?

We have been taught to prioritize *output* over *energy*. How many networking meetings did you have? How many interviews? These are tangible metrics we grasp onto out of (natural) human insecurity and fear. We want proof that we are trying and that we are valuable. I'm here to tell you:

You are inherently worthy.
You matter, no matter what.

We want a job title or romantic partner to make us enough. We want to use our output to signal our value. This strategy fails every time because the only way to cultivate a lasting sense of self-worth is from the inside out by focusing on our energy and how we *feel* instead of our *external output*.

Instead of glorifying or prioritizing your output above all else, turn your gaze inward. If you achieve your goals but are miserable, what's the point?

## Allow Your Energy to Guide Your Choices

Your energy, in bread crumb form and otherwise, is like a secret weapon that will guide you toward your gifts. Begin to notice how you *feel* before, during, and after an activity or conversation. How does your heart feel? Are you energized or depleted? Do you need to rest before moving on?

Years ago, the writer Christine Miserandino shared a blog post that went viral. Christine was sitting in a restaurant when a friend asked what it was like to have lupus. Christine picked up a bunch of spoons from different tables and explained that, if each spoon were a unit of energy, a typical person may have fifty spoons when they wake up in the morning. They spend those spoons on everyday activities such as showering, making breakfast for their kids, getting dressed, driving to work. By the end of the day, most people have five or ten spoons left to talk with their partner, go for a walk, or play with their kids. Christine, however, didn't wake up with fifty spoons.[3]

Christine was forced to make decisions about what her culture said was the right way of being (high productivity, never sleep, go-go-go, busy as a badge of honor) versus what her body would let her do. She had to choose less in terms of traditional output, but this forced her to focus on what truly matters. As a simple way to track your energy, when you're doing anything—working, cleaning the house, spending time with your partner or kids—simply notice: How are your spoons? Being around some people will give you spoons, others take spoons. If you are an introvert, it probably takes spoons to be around a lot of people. If you are an extrovert, that same situation may give you spoons. If you're overwhelmed or exhausted, it means you're giving away more spoons than you're gathering. Period.

Now you have a clear plan to begin following your energetic bread crumbs. This is deep, important work you're doing. Be gentle with yourself and give yourself lots of encouragement. It isn't easy to face your pain, come into awareness, and begin something new.

# FLIP THE SWITCH

## Journaling Prompts: Energy Audit

For the next week, each night before you go to bed, spend five minutes journaling on the following questions:

What gave me the most energy today?

What did I do today that left me with more energy at the end of the activity than I started with?

What specifically energized me about a certain person or situation?

What drained my energy today?

As you do the Energy Audit and begin following your energetic bread crumbs, you'll naturally find yourself in environments that bring out the best in you.[4]

## Soul Symbol

## IX
(pronounced ee'sh)

This symbol represents heart knowing and the magic that occurs when you let go of the rational, controlling, egoic mind. Magic comes not from action but from a quality of perception that exists at a higher frequency. Breathe in and out deeply while gazing at this symbol as you repeat: *I open myself to the unfolding mystery, unseen forces, and heart wisdom.*

I breathe in and surrender to my heart knowing, I breathe out and let go of my mind's illusion of control.

I say yes to magic and my heart's guidance.

*Chapter 4*

# DISCOVER YOUR SUPERPOWER

When I took a leap of faith and quit my job with nothing planned, I felt terrified and exhilarated at the same time. I was like a teenager who broke curfew and was speeding down the highway, giggling at her stolen freedom but scared to death of getting caught—*I was free! Was I free? Oh my god, now what?* I had chosen my soul's longings over my ego's demands, and the vast unknown of it all felt overwhelming and scary.

According to NASA, when an astronaut comes untethered from their spaceship, their sense of orientation gets confused because the vestibular system can no longer differentiate between the ground and the sky.[1] There's no gravity to tell them which way is down. Similarly, when you let go of who you *thought* you should be to discover who you *really* are, the gravitational pull of your own narratives, society's norms, and your family's beliefs no longer anchor your identity. You're free to determine your own truth, and this can be deeply disorienting.

Often we stay inside the safe little box we create with our families, friends, colleagues, and society because it feels comfortable and secure. Sure, maybe the box requires us to stay small in order to fit, but at least we know where the walls begin and end. Everyone else seems to approve of and understand our box. When an incident or a collection of impulses finally prompts us to poke our head out, we feel understandably vulnerable. On a physiological level, our reptilian brain goes on high alert, and we can actually feel like we're in danger. I won't sugarcoat it: whether you're searching for meaningful work, recovering from a divorce or another major loss, or wondering what's next, these periods of upheaval can be scary stuff. A key step in overcoming those fears is gaining clarity on your strengths and unique abilities, so you have something to tether yourself to as you seek The Soul Solution.

In his book *The Big Leap*, psychologist and personal growth expert Gay Hendricks shares how we all have a Zone of Genius. When you're in your Zone of Genius, time goes by quickly, "work doesn't feel like work,"[2] you feel in flow, and you often have more energy at the end of an activity or conversation than you did at the beginning. Reading *The Big Leap* was pivotal during my own career transition, as it encouraged me to begin noticing what I was uniquely suited to do and which people, activities, and experiences energized me. Many years later, I discovered The Native Genius® Method, created by my now dear friend and colleague, Kristen Wheeler. The Native Genius® Method, which helps people find and use their innate gifts, also influenced me tremendously, and I have watched how it has impacted the lives of women I've supported because it is so distilled and actionable. This chapter is my attempt to honor and share Gay and Kristen's work with you, dear reader, because of how important I believe it to be when it comes to living a life aligned with your True Self.

## Play to Your Strengths

Here's a crazy statistic: Gallup asked over ten million people worldwide if they agree with the statement "At work, I have the opportunity to do what I do best every day." Only one-third of people strongly agreed! The survey also found that people who get to focus on their strengths every day are **six times as likely to be engaged in their jobs** and **three times as likely to report having an excellent quality of life in general**.[3] As Kristen Wheeler taught me, this research gives powerful credibility to our deepest longings.

There are many useful tools to help you begin to determine your strengths and what energizes you. Additional resources you may find useful are The Native Genius® Method, the StrengthsFinder 2.0 assessment, and the Enneagram (all referenced at the end of this book).

## What Is Your Zone of Genius?

In *The Big Leap*, Gay Hendricks explains that our activities in the world occur in four main zones: the Zone of Incompetence, the Zone of Competence, the Zone of Excellence, and the Zone of Genius.[4] The Zone of Genius refers to those activities that you are uniquely suited for. You can begin to discover your Zone of Genius simply by **paying attention**. Think of it like peeling back the layers of an onion as you continually ask yourself, *What am I uniquely suited to do?*

That's what my client Tanisha did with the help of the Energy Audit. If you remember from chapter 3, this process involves tracking daily activities and noting which situations, people, and experiences increase your energy and which drain it. Tanisha felt trapped as the CEO of her family business. As part of her audit, I suggested that she journal about her energetic bread crumbs and unique gifts using the prompts "What brings you energy? What makes you feel alive that comes naturally and easily to you?" Tanisha was surprised to discover how much she liked and excelled at being on corporate boards. (This process of noticing how energetic bread crumbs reflect your unique genius was inspired by the Native Genius® Method.[5])

Next, we worked on figuring out *why* Tanisha was good at it. She journaled on the question "What specifically are you doing during board meetings that makes you so effective?" Having grown up in a neighborhood and community that was very different from her family of origin, Tanisha realized she had gained unique insight into disparate groups and perspectives. Journaling on what makes her most effective, Tanisha wrote, "I'm good at creating change by challenging with love. I can speak truth to power, but in a way that's nonthreatening. I like to stand on the lines of difference, whether racial or gender-based. I'm good at standing in that in-between space and translating." Wow! Can't you feel her genius emanating from those words?

Tanisha came up with a new term to describe her unique gifts: "**Standing in the gray zone as an ambassador of light.**" Equipped with these new insights, she began to carve out roles in diversity and inclusion that brought true joy and impact to her career and life overall.

## Quick Soul Tip

Answer these genius-clarifying statements from *The Big Leap*:

What do I most love to do? (I love it so much I can do it for long stretches of time without getting tired or bored.)

What work do I do that doesn't seem like work?

In my work, what produces the highest ratio of abundance and satisfaction to amount of time spent?

One of my unique abilities is . . .

I'm at my best when I'm . . .

Now go a little deeper by answering:

When I'm at my best, the exact thing I'm doing is . . .

Go even deeper by answering:

When I'm doing that, the thing I love most about it is . . .[6]

Bonus:

Without doing or saying anything, people tell me that my presence makes them feel . . .

As you continue to get curious, it's like you're gently removing layers of sediment from a precious gemstone. Each statement, completed with genuine openness and curiosity, brings your sparkle closer to the surface. Don't worry too much about having a neat little descriptor for your Zone of Genius. What's important is spending time getting to know your particular facets, exploring how they look and feel.

### You Will Take Your Genius for Granted

It's normal to discount your Zone of Genius because it comes so naturally to you. You may be oblivious that you're even using it. "[We're taught] to believe it should be hard to do something well," said Gemma, a client of mine.

"That was the biggest switch for me. Oh, you mean this stuff that I find so obviously easy is not obviously easy for everyone else?" Our greatest gifts hide in plain sight because they're so integral to us.

I spent a lot of time trying to encapsulate my Zone of Genius into a neat little phrase. The overachiever in me wanted to distill it down so it felt easier to understand. I've seen this desire to concisely articulate their Zone of Genius trip up many women. For some, it's illuminating to put words to their Zone of Genius. For others, it feels like a stressful homework assignment because the answer is amorphous. If you're spinning your wheels trying to define it, and that feels bad, let it go. Focus on feeling good and paying attention to your energetic bread crumbs and flow so you can recognize what's already a part of you.

Your genius comes down to a quality of being that you bring everywhere you go and that shines most brightly when you're at your best. For example, people often say that my sister, a professional photographer, makes them feel "safe," both when taking their picture and in conversation about their lives. She's nonjudgmental, and there's something about her presence that makes people feel okay to open up. It's not that she does anything overt in her actions, but her *essence* conveys an important message to everyone around her. That inherent quality has served her incredibly well. She's able to capture beautiful and vulnerable moments because her clients feel secure with her behind the lens.

What does your essence convey? I've been told my energy lifts people up and inspires them. I'm able to use my energy as a catalyst for optimism and transformation in others. While my sister's essence or soul signature makes people feel safe, mine makes them feel buoyed. At its deepest level, your Zone of Genius emanates from your one-of-a-kind essence, a quality that's inherent to you.

## The Zone of Incompetence

Another helpful strategy to identify your Zone of Genius is to start noticing when you're *not* in that zone. As you begin the search for your genius, it's often easier to notice when you're off track than when you're on. "When I'm not in my Zone of Genius, things definitely take longer and it's more of a slog," my client Amy shared.

The Zone of Incompetence includes everything you're not good at. Many brilliant women waste precious time, energy, and resources doing things they'd be better off delegating. I recently spent hours trying to hand-draw the Mayan symbols in this book only to discover my publisher's art department could complete this task in a fraction of the time.

If you feel dread, boredom, or discomfort with a task, chances are you may have found your Zone of Incompetence. Sometimes we procrastinate, bury our heads in the sand, and ignore important situations (managing our finances, relationships, etc.) because of the shame and overwhelm we feel in our Zone of Incompetence.

How often do you attempt a task outside your wheelhouse or agree to something you dread out of obligation, guilt, or fatigue with the hassle of offloading the chore to someone else? When you let go of things in your Zone of Incompetence, a tremendous weight is lifted. As you start outsourcing or avoiding these tasks altogether, you'll get a boost of energy that you can apply to those activities that make you feel alive.

Household chores often fall in this zone. "My Zone of Incompetence is definitely cooking!" one client shared. "I used to think I *should* cook home-made meals. I had internalized the cultural message saying that's what a mom does. When I finally just gave up, I got so much energy back! Not just the time cooking but also the psychological drain."

When you find yourself in your Zone of Incompetence, there's one important question you need to answer:

Is this a skill or activity that is
important to me to learn?

## The Zone of Incompetence = Shame Trigger

Many perfectionistic women feel discomfort in the Zone of Incompetence. "It's like I believe I should be good at everything," Tanisha shared, "and when I'm not, I feel shame about myself."

Occasionally you'll decide to turn a Zone of Incompetence into a hobby—for example, you'll learn a new skill such as playing guitar or coding even if it's uncomfortable and you don't have a natural talent. In these situations, it's helpful to recognize that shame and overwhelm may be a part **of your learning curve.** And that's okay!

Or perhaps you have a job you love, but it has challenging elements. You may turn an incompetence into a competence to meet your broader goals. Steer yourself toward the activities in your Zone of Genius *as much as possible.* Delegate the rest *as much as possible.*

At a women's leadership event in Austin, Texas, one woman shyly raised her hand and said, "I just realized I don't have any hobbies. I thought about taking a painting class, but I hate being bad at things, so I just never started." We miss out on so much creativity and joy when we don't allow ourselves to be incompetent long enough to discover pleasure.

Remember, this is a work in progress. *You* are a work in progress. With practice and intention, you can begin spending more time in your Zone of Genius.

## The Zone of Competence

The Zone of Competence includes tasks for which you have competence but not excellence. Many successful women agree to do things they don't want to do because they know they can, they don't want to let others down, or they relish feeling in control. There's nothing wrong with wanting to feel competent, except when it means you're missing out on your Zone of Genius. And the more competent you show yourself to be, the more others will ask you to continue.

Start by asking yourself, *Hmm, where in my life am I stuck in my Zone of Competence? How does it feel?*

And then journal on this question inspired by *The Big Leap*: "If you could stop doing that sort of thing, what would it free up time for you to do?"[7]

## The Zone of Excellence (aka Genius Counterfeit)

The Zone of Excellence is often the trickiest area for driven women. The Zone of Excellence includes activities at which you excel but that don't deeply satisfy you. One of my clients calls it the "Genius Counterfeit Zone" because it keeps presenting itself as her genius but it doesn't actually feel that good.

You might be well compensated for spending time in your Zone of Excellence, receiving material rewards and copious approval. But no matter how much praise or money you collect, something feels off. "When I get stuck in my Zone of Excellence, it's subtle and insidious," said my client Marjorie. "Versus when I'm in my Zone of Genius, I'm honoring myself and listening at a deep level. I have a sense that I'm moving things forward on behalf of others in a way that's beyond what I can immediately see." We all get sucked into the Zone of Excellence because our egos enjoy validation and praise. Don't beat yourself up about it. Just notice when you're there and think about making a different choice about how you spend your time.

## The Competence Trap (and How to Avoid It)

If you've been chasing gold stars most of your life, chances are you've ended up in what Gay Hendricks calls the "Competence Trap."[8] Because we long for validation, safety, and belonging, we stay in jobs and dynamics that don't speak to our souls, and we miss out on our Zone of Genius.

My client Liz is a perfect example. She gave up her job as an attorney to stay home with her kids. When her third child was three, she began to feel the urge to return to work. Her old firm made an offer but, working with me, she realized she didn't want to be a lawyer anymore. Out of financial need, and with a heavy heart, she took a part-time job at the firm. She wasn't ready to leave her kids, wasn't inspired by the work, and since she hadn't offloaded enough tasks at home, resentments started to pile up in her marriage. In the end, she learned how awful it was to say yes when she really meant no. By living through the pain of disregarding her inner voice, Liz realized she needed to honor her needs and be willing to disappoint others, no matter how tough it felt. Finally, she was able to officially close the door and begin pursuing work she enjoyed.

If you slip up and find yourself tempted back into the Competence Trap, be kind and gentle with yourself. Liz eventually figured it out, and you will too. Sometimes we need to take baby steps toward our Zone of Genius. Other times we make quantum leaps forward. All that matters is that you continually tune in to how you feel, notice when you're stuck outside your Zone of Genius, and take steps to course correct.

### Red-Flag Moments = "Should"

How do you get out of the Competence Trap? First, recognize when you're in it. At some point, I noticed a pattern in my life: every time I was *not* in my Zone of Genius—whether I got stuck in Excellence, Competence, or Incompetence—a *should* would always pop up. Through my work with clients, I noticed this pattern in their lives as well.

If you find yourself saying any of the following as the *only* reason why you are taking on a task or role, it may be a sign you are stuck in the Competence Trap:

> *I should do it.*
>
> *I owe them.*
>
> *I don't want to let them down.*
>
> *It's not hard for me, so I'm happy to do it.*
>
> *They need me.*
>
> *It pays well, and I'm good at it, so I may as well.*
>
> *I can do a good job, so I should.*
>
> *If I want to get to XXX, I have to do YYY.*

If you notice yourself thinking these things, stop and ask, *Am I in my Zone of Genius?* Just because you *can* do something doesn't mean you *should.* Instead, ask yourself, *Hmmm, what am I drawn to right now?* Try doing something just for the fun of it. Our current culture, especially in the West, tends to ignore or devalue activities that are purely for pleasure or curiosity. But, as Kristen Wheeler points out, "these nascent, seemingly 'useless' interests can grow into your greatest gifts." Following these interests can also show you what it's like to feel good, helping you make choices to support your authentic self-expression going forward.

## Outdated Roles—Staying Stuck

In addition to the Competence Trap, women are often coerced into outdated and prescriptive roles that keep them locked outside their Zone of Genius. Research shows women are more likely than men to be asked to do tasks at work that don't lead to advancement, such as organize the holiday party, buy a cake for someone's birthday, book a conference room to celebrate, or perform menial administrative tasks such as taking notes in a meeting.[9] This happens with domestic chores as well. Maybe you feel compelled by societal or cultural expectations to make homemade cookies for the bake sale or to fold the laundry rather than asking your partner to step in. By agreeing to these tasks, we inadvertently perpetuate the problem.

We've come by this pattern honestly—and we can change it. We can say no. We can ask for more. We can reach our full potential instead.

One of my girlfriends loved making homemade purees for her baby. I'd rather stick an ice pick in my eye (and put a fork in my other eye rather than have to clean the blender afterward), but I love taking my kids on hikes, baking, and doing craft projects with them. Start to notice what makes you feel alive or which tasks you actually don't mind.[10] As you give yourself permission to focus on those activities in your Zone of Genius and let other things go, you'll feel greater satisfaction overall.

## Carve Out Your Own Role

When you pay attention to your Zone of Genius, you may carve out roles within your organization and home life that are new and different. Allow yourself to think outside the box; don't just default to what others expect. No one else is just like you, so your contributions may not fit into the standard job description. That's okay. The more you can open yourself to exploration outside the standard confines, the easier it will be for you to find The Soul Solution.

When I worked as an investor in consumer products, part of my job was to attend trade shows, such as Expo West, to meet with entrepreneurs and source new investment opportunities. That was my dream come true: I got paid to walk around sampling gluten-free cookies while having conversations with fascinating CEOs. One year, after attending the trade show, my boss pulled me aside to say that the partners thought I had been the most productive employee at the event. It was a big compliment.

Here's the thing: I loved that part of my job! Connection is one of my core values, and I enjoy discovering new products and having energizing conversations with entrepreneurs. Yet it never occurred to me to request that I spend *more time* doing this aspect of my job. In hindsight I can see that I would have been a greater asset to our firm if I had. This is a natural mistake a lot of us make because we've been conditioned to follow the rules.

You have more room than you realize to carve out your niche, even within a big organization. If there's something you're interested in, volunteer your time. Get to know the project or team lead and see how you can add value. Pay attention to your *energy* as you contribute. I guarantee that if you're enjoying yourself and spending time in your Zone of Genius, you'll have a positive impact, and other people will want to expand your role as well.

# FLIP THE SWITCH

## Friends and Family Genius Survey: Uncovering Your True Gifts and Impact

Often our greatest gifts are so much a natural part of who we are that we don't notice them. Since these behaviors are so intrinsic, our friends, family, and colleagues (who don't have the same gifts) can see them more clearly than we can. This is why it can be so helpful to hear their reflections on the essence of us and the impact we have on others.

Speak to at least three to five people you're close with—people who know you very well. Include at least one work colleague, if possible. Explain that you're trying to discover things that you're naturally good at doing and that you enjoy. Ask the following questions:

- What is the most impactful gift or thing that I do that has value for others or an organization? What do you think I'm really good at?

- What do I do well, no matter what environment I'm in?

- What is unique about how I do this or how I show up? How is it distinctive from other people?

- What is the biggest impact or benefit it has for other individuals or an organization?

- What do you get from me as a friend/family member/ colleague that you don't get from anyone else?

- Is there anything else we haven't covered yet to describe the impact I make on you or the organization?

Take notes in your Soul Solution Journal, notice themes, and see how the answers compare with your Energy Audit.

## Go Deeper: Genius Journaling

Journal on these questions for each zone to spotlight red flags that signify when you've strayed. *(There is a free guided meditation to take you through these practices at* vanessaloder.com/book.*)*

**Zone of Genius:** Think of a time in the recent past when you were in your Zone of Genius, doing something that comes naturally to you and you're uniquely suited to do. What were you doing? What do you see, hear, smell, sense? What does it *feel* like in your body when you're operating from your Zone of Genius?

**Zone of Excellence:** Think of a time when you were in your Zone of Excellence, doing something at which you excel and are well compensated or rewarded for doing but that doesn't deeply satisfy you. What were you doing? What do you see, hear, smell, sense? What does it *feel* like in your body when you're operating from your Zone of Excellence?

**Zone of Competence:** Think of a time when you were in your Zone of Competence, doing something that you're capable of but don't excel at. What were you doing? What do you see, hear, smell, sense? What does it *feel* like in your body when you're operating from your Zone of Competence?

**Zone of Incompetence:** Think of a time when you were in your Zone of Incompetence, doing something that you're not good at. What were you doing? What do you see, hear, smell, sense? What does it *feel* like in your body when you're operating from your Zone of Incompetence?

Based on your new insights, what will you let go of, delegate, or outsource? What will you keep, add, or include more of?

## Soul Symbol

## Dreamer and Dreamed

This symbol represents your personal dream that is woven together by your unique meaning and purpose in this lifetime. Breathe in and out deeply while gazing at this symbol and ask yourself, *What brings me joy? What would I like? What is the new dream I want to bring to life?*

I am the dreamer and the mythmaker of my life.

I follow my imagination to create a new reality for myself.

# Chapter 5

# CHASING GOLD STANDARDS VERSUS YOUR TRUE NORTH STAR

**M**y former client Melanie is a smart cookie with a fancy pedigree. She went to Stanford, worked in wealth management at Goldman Sachs, and graduated from law school at the top of her class before choosing a career in litigation. Yet at thirty-five, she found herself involuntarily single, unemployed after layoffs, and living at home with her parents.

After a few weeks of wallowing in pints of ice cream and television streaming binges, Melanie took an honest look in the mirror and what she saw surprised her: She realized her goal in life wasn't to be the best litigator in the world. What she really wanted was to have a husband, kids, and work that made her happy. After reading a blog I wrote about energetic bread crumbs, Melanie decided to reach out to me. "I used to think about my goals in terms of the job itself—what's the best title, what's the highest level?" she said. "But recently I realized that's not making me happy. I love writing and being part of a close-knit team. But if you're a junior litigator at a big firm, you're not doing writing. It's become ingrained in me that my worth is tied to the job. But I don't want that to be the only criteria anymore, and I want someone I trust to say it's okay to do it this other way."

Melanie followed up on a hunch she had to contact a former colleague about bankruptcy law, but she still doubted her impulses.

Because she loves writing, I asked Melanie to listen to my Future Self Guided Visualization and then write out a script for her ideal life, as if she were both the director and screenwriter of her own imagined story.[1] In her screenplay, the character of Melanie was living in the West Village with a great romantic partner, walking to work with a latte. On the weekends, she read at her kitchen table and did crossword puzzles with her boyfriend.

Once Melanie finished writing, she realized that her options were broader than she'd realized. "I'm still moving forward with my job search in New York, but I feel so much less anxious about finding the perfect job or role," she explained. "It's just one part of my entire life. Before, I was so hung up on [being] a litigator. I felt limited, but then I realized **I painted myself into that corner.** I created this myth that my job is the be-all and end-all. **And I can uncreate that myth.**"

Writing her life script helped Melanie let go of impossible ideals and feel a playful sense of control as she tapped into her unique desires.

When Melanie followed her energetic bread crumbs, she found herself on a path more aligned with her True Self. She was able to shed some of the pressures we feel as women to please others. As she began learning about bankruptcy law, she said her whole body felt "excited and animated." At times, her ego dropped in and created doubt around prestige and old standards for success, and she even had to take a small break from some negative friends. But in the end, she followed her bread crumbs to a new job in New York despite a down economy, and she felt inspired to apply the same self-honoring attitude to her personal life.

It's easy to feel trapped on a hamster wheel and lose sight of the big picture. And as "good girls" who follow the rules, we can get stuck chasing traditional goals that don't feed our souls. Our culture is geared toward advancement without questioning if that satisfies our deeper desires or overall well-being. Here's the truth:

Advancement without alignment does
not feel good (eventually).

If you're focused on advancement without considering your core values, unique gifts, and a bigger "Why?" you will end up unfulfilled. If you pursue goals without attuning to your well-being and authentic needs, you will wind up burned out. Climbing another rung of someone else's ladder may offer a sense of forward momentum, but eventually it feels hollow. I know from personal and professional experience. It's essential to **focus on feeling good** as we pursue our desires.

After you come into awareness about what's *not* working and begin listening to your soul's whispers, the next step on your Soul Solution journey is to begin to understand your power as a creator and what effective creation is all about. But first it can be helpful to recognize and release outdated obstacles. We need to talk about the old system of creation that includes traditional goal setting, rigid beliefs based on a linear model of progression, and a myopic, patriarchal, and egoic definition of success. (Yup, I said it.)

Our culture has laid out, and we as women have internalized, a series of ideals that I refer to as the "Gold Standards." We feel tremendous pressure to meet the Gold Standards regardless of whether they're nourishing us as individuals. Unwinding society's implicit definitions of success, beauty, health, parenting, and more is a necessary step in figuring out whether you're chasing your dreams or someone else's.

## Whose Dreams Are You Chasing?

We all have an inner compass. Society's compass (based on the Gold Standards) does not usually agree with our inner compass. When we follow society's compass, we do and say things that don't feel good. We end up unfulfilled. The way we set goals is fundamentally flawed in our culture today because we encourage everyone to chase a standard set of ideals rather than discovering their own True North Star. In almost all areas of our lives—career, relationships, health, beauty, spirituality, religion, and more—we chase standards without questioning who set them, whether they serve us, and how we feel in the pursuit and attainment of them.

If, like me, you are a driven woman who relishes the feeling of satisfaction from a job well done, I invite you to pause and get genuinely curious about who has influenced your agenda. Your soul or your ego? Are you following your inner truth or society's norms?

Here in the United States, we live in a consumerist, capitalist patriarchy. Judgment aside, if consumerism and patriarchy don't give you the warm fuzzies or nurture your inner truth, then you'll need to forge your own authentic path, which is particularly tricky since our culture also doesn't teach us, as women, to trust ourselves.

## The Myth of the Gold Standard

One example of inauthentic and self-negating goal-chasing is how much time women spend trying to achieve an unrealistic Western Gold Standard of Beauty (skinny, white, young-looking, with copious amounts of hair—but only on your head). We also fold laundry, schedule the kids' doctor's appointments, organize birthday parties, volunteer at the kids' school, plan the playdates, and pack the snacks in an unconscious attempt to meet some outdated 1950s definition of a Gold Standard Mother. We schedule date nights, wear fancy underwear, and have sex even when we're tired or resentful, all to be the Gold Standard Wife or Partner. And, of course, we kill ourselves at the office, working nights and weekends, all to be the Gold Standard Employee or Entrepreneur. It's exhausting just to list these, let alone to live them.

This myth that we should conform to uniform standards is the main source of the pressure for perfection that many women feel. We women create "perfect pictures" in our minds based on these singular ideals, derived from social media, advertising, family norms, and broader cultural messaging, and then we beat ourselves up when we fail to match those images. This vicious cycle of feeling the pressure to meet multiple Gold Standards and the shame when we fall short is one of the main causes of today's rampant burnout and overwhelm.

This is why it's so important to acknowledge the external messaging that we have inadvertently internalized. We're not crazy. We didn't become perfectionists overnight in a vacuum. Society taught us this. Skim any magazine and you'll see the evidence. For example, while no one explicitly sat me down and told me to lose the baby weight in four months, it was inferred all over the place: *Look at these moms at the beach in bikinis with newborns! Gisele did it, and you can too!* When our culture refuses to honor exhausted moms with bags under their eyes and folds of flab, we are subtly being told to hide our truth as well. And the pressure isn't unique to the beauty and parenting industries. At many workplaces, employees are rewarded for 24/7 accessibility, even if that means being on their phones during dinner with loved ones. Reclaiming our intrinsic feminine power must include refusing to play by the rules of any dissatisfying or exhausting game.

Gold Standards of Achievement from earning a high GPA to getting a promotion can be worthwhile objectives. The rub comes when you are not intrinsically inspired but instead doggedly pursue these aims merely to accumulate more accolades. You become dependent on the Gold Standards themselves rather than enjoying the activities for their own sake.

If you're like me, your sense of self-worth and identity have probably become somewhat dependent on Gold Standards: "I *am* a doctor." "I *am* athletic." "I *am* a caring sister." But these arbitrary standards and metrics have nothing to do with you as a unique soul. And it's an unwinnable game because Gold Standards keep getting higher. (And aging is inevitable, so we're really in a pickle there!)

Gold Standards reflect what our society currently deems important and valuable but neglect to offer validity to many important roles historically performed by women, such as caregiving and community building. This means if you choose that kind of work, you're likely to feel undervalued or even invisible—because you are.

Aside from feeling as though we're not enough, the real loss in the process of chasing Gold Standards is that we clamp down on important aspects of self. Our creativity. Our wildness. Our authentic, messy humanness. Our feminine wisdom and intuition. Our own needs and desires. Our unique essence. By following other people's notions of what constitutes a Gold Standard, we're upholding the very system that depletes us. If we want to create structural change, we must learn to relinquish these ideals, even if it challenges our previous sense of self-worth. At their core, Gold Standards keep women small, and we are way too powerful for that nonsense.

## Gold Standards Squash Creativity

When our eight-year-old daughter makes her bed, she creates these elaborate arrangements. Her stuffies (in order of favorites and grouped by "family") sit regally on a throne made of her fuzzy pillow, sequined unicorn flip pillow, and mermaid-tail blanket. To top it all off, she arranges a unicorn blanket (You can *never* have too many unicorns. Never.) in a neat rectangle at the foot of the bed for our (real, not stuffed) cat to sleep on.

Instead of rewarding our daughter for simply making her bed, which would have incentivized her to meet the goal in the most traditional way, with hospital corners and such, we celebrate her unique arrangements as much as possible to encourage her to express her creativity and savor the experience. In a global economy that is now reliant on creative problem-solving, stifling creativity is a serious issue. Teaching everyone to stay in line and follow a linear path forward is neither serving our economy's larger objectives nor our individual self-expression and well-being.

## Women and the Gold Standard of Pleasing Others

Two implicit Gold Standards women have been programmed to meet are being liked and taking care of others. As a result, we're often more loyal to the needs and opinions of others than to our own deeper wants.

As infants, our survival is utterly dependent on the attention and approval of the adults around us. As we grow up, we begin twisting ourselves into pretzels to maintain that, fitting into the mold they lay out. We attune ourselves to the expectations of others. (If you're born in a female or other marginalized body, you sign up for the advanced placement (AP) version of this course.)

From the moment of your birth, people begin projecting their dreams, unmet needs, and beliefs onto you. Whether it's your dad's dashed aspirations of being a star athlete; or your culture's indoctrination that the only jobs worth pursuing are in medicine, law, or business; or your family's difficulties with financial stability that forged a strong desire in you to be self-sufficient, we've all been shaped by our backgrounds in profound ways that have little to do with our individual strengths or needs.

I still inadvertently chase Gold Standards all the time. When I notice myself going astray, I take steps to return home. Heck, I caught myself chasing a Gold Standard with the cover design on this very book! One design option was a black cover that looked "smart" and authoritative, and another option was bright and colorful and felt more soul-based. I was tempted to choose the black cover for ego-driven reasons. (*The experts say it could appeal to a broader demographic. Another book with a similar design was a NYT best seller!*) But when I tuned in to my body, heart, and intuition, the bright cover felt more energizing and aligned with the messages in the book. (Plus my community voted it their favorite!) After meditating and noticing how each book cover design felt in my body, my choice became clear. I course-corrected and honored what felt right.

When I notice my ego running rampant, instead of beating myself up, I do my best to accept that, as the popular saying goes, this is what it means to be a spiritual being having a human experience. We have *both* a soul and an ego, and we get to choose which one has the steering wheel. Chasing Gold Standards even when it makes you miserable doesn't make you a bad person. It just makes you an unaware person living in the collective trance. If you're here now, it's because you are ready to wake up and come home to you.

## Choose *Feeling Good* Instead of *Should*

After too long chasing other people's dreams, shoulds, and expectations, you may begin to ask yourself, *What is it all for? What do I really want?*

This is the moment when your disillusion with the Gold Standards can help you pivot toward The Soul Solution and discover your True North Star. You can begin to get there by noticing when you are choosing *should* over *feeling good.*

Does this sound familiar?

*I should stay at my current job because it pays well.*

*I should go to my friend's party even though I'm exhausted.*

*I should volunteer at my kids' school.*

*I should go to this interview to explore my options, even though I don't want the job.*

In the last chapter, we talked about how there is often a "should" behind any choice that takes you outside of your Zone of Genius. To continue peeling back these layers, start to notice when you are doing something only out of guilt, obligation, or to be liked and viewed favorably.

## *Quick Soul Tip*

Make a list of the biggest shoulds that currently run your life. Which of these are you ready to let go of? For each should, write down the *desire* that is underneath the should. Does the desire point to a larger core value? Think of at least one idea for what would *feel good* in that particular situation. Act on what feels good instead of the should.

### Examples:

*I should lose five pounds.*

**Desire or core value:** I want to feel good in my body. Core values = energized and confident.

**What feels good?** I feel good when I move my body. I feel good when I eat foods that nourish my body.

**Action:** Dance to energizing music for five to ten minutes.

*I should join that task force at work.*

**Desire or core value:** I want to make an impact. Core value = impact.

**What feels good?** I feel good when I use my unique gifts to contribute to meaningful projects at work.

**Action:** Say no. This project is not meaningful to me, and it does not allow me to use my unique gifts, so I will say no to it.

The next time you are debating whether to take on a new project or role, take a moment to get still. Notice how you feel. Is your body tight, tense, or heavy? Or is it light, open, and relaxed? Put your hand on your heart, inhale deeply into your heart, exhale from your heart. Repeat that a few more times and then ask yourself, *What does my heart want me to do? If I could hear my heart, what would it be saying?*

*Should* is a red flag that indicates we care more about what other people think than what we feel inside. When we say "should," we are choosing to please others over pleasing ourselves. When we do something we don't really want to do, we feel icky or heavy inside. See if you can begin to make "feeling good" the driving motivation behind your choices. Be wild and reckless and free. Say no to the volunteer opportunity, to the extra project at work, to baking those cupcakes from scratch. Instead, go home, light some candles, make yourself a cup of tea, and read a book in your favorite cozy nook. Do whatever pleases *you*. Notice if any guilt crops up, then do it anyway.

## Your True North Star

Unlike Gold Standards, your True North Star is not a singular tangible metric. Instead, it's a beacon you move toward, a compass guiding you forward. Other people may not see or understand your True North Star. **The goodness that will come into your life *is* universal, but the standard of measuring your achievement is not.** Each person is on their own journey with their own unique gifts and lessons. Yet the more you align with your True North Star, the more delight, creativity, abundance, and ease you'll discover.

If, like me, you have been dutifully chasing the Gold Standards most of your life, it can feel daunting to begin discovering and honoring your True North Star. One easy way to start tuning in to your inner compass is to get clear on your core values. As you make consistent choices that align with those values, you will move toward your True North Star. You can use the Values Tool on my website vanessaloder.com/book or simply make a list of the values or qualities of being that matter most to you at this time. Identifying the gap between your actual versus aspirational values can help point you in the direction of where you want to go next. For example, my core values are connection, playfulness, love, spiritual growth, joyful expansion, and uplifting women and girls. When I live according to these values, I feel really good.

Deep down, you know what you need, what pleases you, what feels good. You know when you are inspired to take action and when you need to rest, but you have learned to ignore or override these inner signals. Our broader society supports this suppression, encouraging you to choose their achievement goals over self-care. The mainstream message is not:

*She got still and quiet and found her voice. She took space to come home to herself and honor her innate wisdom and needs. She luxuriated in leisure. She gave her time and energy to caregiving and building community. She prioritized her creativity and pursued her pleasure. She took a risk at work. Let's celebrate and honor her as the titan that she is.*

Only you can determine whether you are on or off track as it relates to pursuing Gold Standards versus your True North Star. Coming back to your core values will help you decipher which track you are on. When you first decide to stop chasing, you may abandon one path only to people-please in other ways. That's what (almost) happened to me. At first, after leaving my job, I pursued opportunities that were adjacent to my current career; I was dipping my toe into the frigid water of change without fully diving in. But my ideas were based on making money, not inspiration, and they weren't bringing me joy. I was still using the wrong metrics of success. My compass was so tuned in to what society deemed important that, even though I craved something more, I had no idea how to follow the guidance of my True North Star.

But then I remembered the expression "If you keep doing what you've always done, you'll keep getting what you've always got." While muddling through this dilemma on a hike by the beach, a fully formed insight came *through* me: *My entire life, I've been following my ego, my mind, and my wallet instead of my heart or intuition. Maybe that's why I'm unfulfilled.*

So I began following my energetic bread crumbs, and within two weeks, several people reached out to me for coaching advice because they wanted to quit *their* jobs. I began coaching people one-on-one, but then I noticed I was even more energized working in groups. I also identified uplifting women and girls as one of my core values and something I wanted to pursue with my work. Within a few months I realized I wanted to run group coaching programs and retreats for women navigating career transitions. Things fell into place with a grace and ease I had never experienced.

Maybe you don't feel financially stable enough to quit your job or take quite that large a step. Don't worry, there are many ways you can move toward your True North Star without a radical life change. The important part is to let yourself do something "just 'cause" you get an inkling about it. Even seemingly mundane actions can become relevant bread crumb moments, such as texting someone with a compliment because you are savoring something you admire about them, picking up a book that calls to you from the bookstore shelf, or following your instinct to speak up in a meeting and then having your contribution turn out to change the meeting for the better.

Ten years later, I am still finding new ways to follow my True North Star. All along, I've continued to honor my core values and follow my heart and body, those sacred places inside of me that house my deeper truth. My intuition has never steered me wrong. My mind still cares about what other people think, gaining prestige, making more money, and scaling my business as fast as possible. None of these things are inherently wrong, but I've learned that if I *only* follow these dictates from my ego, it will not lead to lasting satisfaction.

Now I'm focused on soul-centric (aligned) success. I enjoy trusting my intuition, doing things that make me feel alive, and savoring the results. When I attain this type of "success," it's the best high of my life. The whole enchilada. And I want you to have that enchilada too!

## Find a Bigger Pot

Did you know that plants will grow smaller or larger depending on the size of the pot they are in? Researchers did 3D MRI root scans that showed potted plants use their roots to sense the size of the pot and then grow accordingly. Often when you are stressed, burned out, and exhausted, it's because you are trying to fit into a pot that's too small to hold all of you. You're following Gold Standards instead of your True North Star and not doing what your body needs to feel rested and nourished, and it's taking a toll on your well-being.

As part of The Soul Solution, you may find that some of your containers are too tight and rigid. You need more space to expand and explore. Perhaps it's time to intentionally re-pot into a bigger container that can accommodate all of you (or at least more of you).

# FLIP THE SWITCH

## Clarify Core Values

You can begin to determine your core values by scanning the list below and circling the top ten or twenty values that most resonate for you today. Then try to narrow it down to your top five to ten values. Write these core values on an index card or sticky note and then place it on your nightstand or bathroom mirror. Each morning, read the list and then ask yourself, *How can I live more in alignment with my values of X, Y, and Z today?*

| | |
|---|---|
| Abundance | Competition |
| Attraction | Completion |
| Authenticity | Connection |
| Autonomy | Contribution |
| Awareness | Control |
| Balance | Courage |
| Beauty | Creativity |
| Being the best | Daring |
| Bliss | Decisiveness |
| Boldness | Dependability |
| Camaraderie | Determination |
| Certainty | Dignity |
| Choice | Diligence |
| Clarity | Directness |
| Collaboration | Discipline |
| Commitment | Discovery |
| Community | Ease |
| Compassion | Elegance |

| | |
|---|---|
| Emotions | Health |
| Empathy | Helpfulness |
| Empowerment | Honesty |
| Encouragement | Humility |
| Energy | Humor |
| Enjoyment | Imagination |
| Enthusiasm | Impact |
| Excellence | Improvement |
| Excitement | Independence |
| Experience | Information |
| Experimenting | Innovation |
| Expression | Inspiration |
| Fame | Integrity |
| Family | Intellect |
| Feeling good | Intention |
| Flexibility | Intimacy |
| Flow | Inventiveness |
| Focus | Joy |
| Freedom | Justice |
| Friendship | Kindness |
| Fun | Knowledge |
| Generosity | Leadership |
| Gentleness | Learning |
| Gratitude | Legacy |
| Growth | Liveliness |
| Happiness | Love |
| Harmony | Loyalty |

| | |
|---|---|
| Mastery | Purpose |
| Meaning | Realism |
| Mindfulness | Reason |
| Nature | Recognition |
| Novelty | Relaxation |
| Nurturing | Reputation |
| Openness | Resourcefulness |
| Optimism | Respect |
| Orderliness | Responsibility |
| Originality | Risk taking |
| Outdoors | Romance |
| Ownership | Sacrifice |
| Participation | Satisfaction |
| Passion | Security |
| Patience | Self-expression |
| Peace | Self-reliance |
| Perfection | Sensitivity |
| Persistence | Sensuality |
| Philanthropy | Significance |
| Play | Solitude |
| Playfulness | Spirituality |
| Popularity | Spontaneity |
| Positivity | Stewardship |
| Power | Style |
| Preparedness | Success |
| Privacy | Support |
| Productivity | Teaching |

Traditions                    Variety

Tranquility                   Vitality

Trust                         Vulnerability

Understanding                 Wealth

Upliftment

Feel free to add or make up your own values if something you want is missing from this list!

## Untwist Your Pretzel

It can be liberating to recognize the ways in which you've twisted yourself into a pretzel to appease others rather than stretching gloriously out into your own funky shape.

### Source Your Beliefs Tool

Let's untwist your pretzel by examining your goals and desires. List two to three goals that you have right now in your Soul Solution Journal.

For each goal, now write:

What my mom says about (insert your goal). . .

What my dad says about (insert your goal). . .

What my (insert spouse, friend, sibling, teacher, etc.) says about . . .

What society says about . . .

What X (insert any other influential figure, celebrity, media outlet, or cultural narrative) says about . . .

This will help you begin to identify whose dreams you are really chasing.

You can also answer the questions above in relation to some of your core beliefs about success, money, being a working woman, caregiving, creative pursuits, health, beauty, etc. For example,

What my mom says about working women . . .

What my dad says about working women . . .

What my (insert spouse, friend, sibling, teacher, etc.) says about working women . . .

What society says about working women . . .

What X (list any other influential figure, celebrity, media outlet, or cultural narrative) says about working women . . .

Once you're ready to figure out what *you* (and no one else) want, start small. You don't have to figure out everything at once. Your True North Star can simply help you decide what color pillow you want for the couch or what your body wants for lunch.

If you tune in to your inner guidance system for little choices throughout the day, it will add up to big changes. Those small decisions are significant. These are the moments when we are tempted to rush and ignore the quiet voice inside, override our deeper knowing, and abandon ourselves.

## Shift from Shame and Should to Focus on Feeling Good

Here is a simple tool to peel back the layers of any should and then shift focus to the core feelings you desire underneath. This will help you reframe the goal to focus on what actually matters to you.

One goal or Gold Standard I have been beating myself up about is _____.

One reason I should cut myself some slack in relation to this goal is _____.

What value is this pointing to?

Shift to: How do I really want to *feel*?

Practice: Spend two to three breaths remembering a time in the past when you felt the way you now want to feel. Savor the sensations and let them soak into every cell of your being.

Example—Career

*Nagging Gold Standard: I should be promoted to VP in six months.*

One reason I should cut myself some slack in relation to this goal is _____.

> *Ex: Fewer people got promoted last year, the rush to get promoted is self-created, only one other person has been promoted this quickly.*

What value is this pointing to?

> *Ex: I really want to make a difference at work and feel appreciated for sharing my unique gifts in a useful way.*

> Shift to: I feel confident using my gifts and strengths to have an impact at work.

> Practice: Spend two to three breaths remembering a time in the past when you made an impact while using your unique abilities. Savor the sensations and let them soak into every cell of your being.

Optional

List three things you appreciate that are going well right now in relation to this goal:

1. I had a solid impact at our last companywide meeting when I made that salient point.

2. I connected with a potential mentor at a recent event.

3. This job is showing me what some of my unique gifts have to do with connecting with people across differences. I can take this insight and seek out roles outside of work that enable me to leverage my unique genius more.

## Soul Symbol

## Transparency

This symbol represents letting go of overidentifications, the roles you have been playing, and the false acting that has begun to ring hollow. It is time to undefine the self. Breathe in and out deeply while gazing at this symbol and say to yourself: *I am transparent, free from definition. I am free to explore and play any part at any moment.*

I explore new roles with ease and joy.

I am limitless.

*Chapter 6*

# FROM TUNNEL VISION TO VISIONARY

One very effective way to get what you want in life is to harness the power of the subconscious mind. Here's the crazy thing: our conscious brain (which we *think* is running the show) processes information at a rate of about fifty bits per second, while our unconscious, intuitive nervous system processes information at a rate of eleven *million* bits per second.[1] That means that 95 percent of *all* of our brain activity isn't actually conscious!

Considering that our thoughts create our reality, that's quite a predicament. Fortunately, there are ways to intentionally influence our subconscious mind. Visualization is one powerful tool for linking up the conscious and subconscious. To get a sense of this, close your eyes and picture a yellow flower. Now, see a red bird. (Wait, how are you reading this with your eyes closed? You really are gifted!) But seriously, if you close your eyes again, can you see a red bird?

Nice work! You just did a guided visualization. It's that simple. Most of us were never taught that our subconscious mind doesn't think in language; it responds to images, symbols, and feelings. That's why when you are in a relaxed state, zoning out while driving the car or taking a shower, you have more access to creativity and inspired ideas. The conscious (chattering) mind is not getting in the way, reminding you to pick up the dry cleaning or return a friend's call.

Once you learn visualization techniques, you can apply them to any area of your life. I suggest you start visualizing areas of your life where you have less resistance, where it's easier for you to *believe* and *feel* your desired future state. This will help you gain confidence in these techniques.

There are two types of visioning I've observed in my own life: *Spontaneous (or receptive) visioning* is when a vision comes to you unprompted. It can arrive in a dream, a serendipitous encounter, or by following your soul whispers and energetic bread crumbs. What I call *intentional visioning* is when you have a specific outcome or desired feeling in mind. You already know what you want. We're going to focus on intentional visioning first because it's easier to teach and practice. I'll get to spontaneous visioning later.

Both processes require a level of trust and surrender. You must stop trying to control everything and allow things to unfold while staying in a receptive state. This is not easy when you really want something!

## Seeing and Feeling Your Desired Future

To practice intentional visioning, choose images that represent a desired future scenario or state of being. For example, if I want more intimacy and connection in my marriage, I might visualize my husband and myself laughing together over some shared story. It's important that the images elicit positive feelings. I invite you to play around to see what creates the strongest resonance in your body. How a vision *feels* is more important than *what* you are visualizing.

When I first began using visualization to boost my immune system, the image that popped up *and* that evoked the strongest feelings in my body was of the stormtroopers from *Star Wars* as my white blood cells. I could easily imagine their white uniforms and really *feel* them marching around my body in straight lines, ushering out any disease. Years later, I came to feel that the stormtrooper image was too violent, and it lost its power, which can happen after a lot of repetition. Instead, I transformed the white blood cells into kind but firm Buddhist monks in white robes, gently guiding out any illness and saying, "Now it's time for you to go! You have to leave the temple of Vanessa's body."

So, experiment with the images that work for you and be creative. You are your own best authority. You'll know when you have found a solid visualization because you will *feel* it emotionally and palpably in your body. Sometimes a scene from a movie or something you've experienced in a visceral way in the past can be used to help engage your mind.

A strong visualization uses all five senses, magnifying some more than others. There's no wrong way to do it.

A word of warning: Your mind will come in during the visualization and chatter at you, full of opinions and judgments. Every time I practice, my mind interrupts with thoughts like, *This isn't working. This is weird. Why did you choose stormtroopers, you freak?! They're bad guys.* This doesn't mean you're doing it wrong. It's part of the process. Simply respond, *Thank you for your input, mind, but I've got this*, and gently return to the visualization.

This is why, especially in the beginning, it can be helpful to listen to a guided visualization. Listening to someone else's voice gently giving you instructions can be supportive to the process and help you stay focused. You can access my Guided Visualization to Boost Immunity, Lower Anxiety, and Promote Healing and Future Self Guided Visualization at vanessaloder.com/book.

## Choosing the Motivation Behind Your Goal

When we talk about the soul versus ego, we run the risk of characterizing one as good and the other as bad, particularly if our goal feels financially focused. Instead of judging, simply tune in to how you *feel*. As a simple example: let's say you want a new car. Ask yourself, *Is my primary motivation to keep up with my neighbors?* If your goal originates in fear and lack, it probably won't feel very good. If, on the other hand, you want a new car because it genuinely feels good, you feel safe in it, or you just love how it looks, this desire will feel more aligned. Look at the bigger why or motivation behind what you desire to clarify your alignment.

Rather than accumulating stuff, money, job titles, or accolades, what if the new metric for success was **how good you feel**? Years ago, I set a goal to create a million-dollar business, and I put a lot of pressure on myself to attain it. Every year, when I fell (*really*) short of that lofty goal, I'd beat myself up. That shame spiral paralyzed me so that I didn't take the actions I needed to grow my business.

Everything changed when I stopped focusing on the specific goal that was making me feel miserable and allowed myself to explore the *feelings* behind the goal. *What was the bigger why behind wanting a million-dollar business? How would my life be different if I had it? What feeling was I hoping it would give me?*

I quickly identified one of the core feelings I was hoping for: **luxuriousness**. When I began focusing on *feeling* luxurious in my current daily life, I realized that a supersoft, cozy blanket and fireplace in my living room gave me the same desired feeling without all the hustle. By focusing on the luxury that already surrounded me, I was able to relax in relation to the goal and feel better. Now I have more time with my kids because I'm not putting pressure on myself to work crazy hours, and I have more appreciation for luxury without the complexity of managing more stuff.

In the previous chapter we talked about the Gold Standards myth. We've been led to believe that more is always better. If you've done any previous visioning work, you may have been taught to imagine your goals and repeat affirmations as specifically as possible. In fact, what my clients have found most effective is *not* always setting goals and instead focusing on how you want to *feel* in a broad sense while recognizing that sometimes less is more.

## The Ambitious Shame Spiral

Many perfectionist overachievers quickly set higher and more specific goals, which can backfire as it increases internal pressure and makes it harder to keep your goal truly aligned with your soul.

A common pattern with women in the workplace, at home, and beyond goes something like this:

Phase 1: Set an ambitious and specific goal.

Phase 2: Notice how far your present reality is from the high bar you just set.

Phase 3: Push yourself really hard to meet that high bar.

Phase 4: Become exhausted and discouraged.

Phase 5: Go into a shame spiral when you fail to meet the high bar, or attain the goal but at the detriment of your well-being.

Phase 6: Blame yourself. Compare yourself to others. Give up or double down on pushing yourself even harder next time.

## Is Your Focus on Desire or Lack?

(Hint: your feelings will answer this question every time.)

When I first set my million-dollar goal, I *thought* I was envisioning my ideal future. In reality, instead of feeling the beauty and power of my vision, I was focusing on the painful gap between where I was and where I wanted to be.

If a specific goal triggers you or feels bad, drop it like a hot potato. When specificity causes misery, shame, insecurity, and/or compare despair, it is not serving you. The best thing you can do in these instances is *stop thinking about it*! Seriously. Zoom out with your vision. Get clear on your core desired feelings and the bigger why behind your goal. For example, with my business, instead of focusing on a specific revenue amount, I took a more macro view and focused on how I want to feel energized and playful while uplifting women and creating a global community of like-minded souls. Now *that* feels good!

When you focus on how far you are from your goals, all you can see is what's *not* working. Another sneaky pitfall that puts you in a lacking mindstate is focusing too much on the "how" or the logistics of your goal. To mitigate this pattern of feeling insufficient, focus on what *is* working instead, even if it seems trivial. We dismiss these small wins, but they matter.

When you focus on what *is* working, you align your energy with what you want, build positive momentum, and harness the power of the Law of Attraction. The Law of Attraction is the tendency to draw what we're focusing on into our lives. This works in reverse as well: if you focus on what's *not* going well, you tend to attract more of what you *don't* want. When you become aware of how one thought leads to another, which leads to another, you can interrupt the cycle to focus on more uplifting thoughts and reactions. This not only rewires your brain over time but also helps you manifest more of what you really want in your life!

Here's another fascinating truth: sometimes things that *don't* feel good feel so *normal* that we keep doing them anyway. In these instances, you can find The Soul Solution by focusing on your desired feelings instead. For example, let's say you have a long-standing habit of criticizing your romantic partner. It feels bad, but it has become habitual and happens automatically. The next time you catch yourself in judgment mode, try to interrupt the cycle by telling yourself, *I commit to focusing on the good I already have in my romantic partnership*, then focus on one to three things you can appreciate about your partner or your relationship. Imagine how you want to feel in a relationship and try to remember times when you felt that way in the past.

## When All Else Fails, Just Go to Sleep

What if you can't access good feelings?

Sometimes, when you're having a really bad day, you may feel so stuck that you can't shift your energy. It may not be until you fall asleep that you can hit the reset button. Taking a nap or going to bed is actually a viable solution when you feel terrible because sleep shifts you back into neutral.

In fact, one of the most potent times for visualization is in bed at night, right before drifting off to sleep. Some researchers suggest that the last minute before you fall asleep stays in your subconscious mind for up to seven hours![2] This is a great time to connect with your future self.

## Meet Your Future Self

Research has repeatedly shown that visualizing and connecting with "our best possible future self" makes us happier and more optimistic. It can also influence our behavior and help us make healthy choices that are aligned with our longer-term goals.[3]

A couple of years ago, my client Sameera called me and breathlessly exclaimed, "The visualization we did at your retreat just came true in eerie detail!" When we met, Sameera was feeling burned out and wanted to make a career shift. She followed her energetic bread crumbs to design school and was on her way to interview for a new job when she found herself in an all-white office building with a unique architectural design that *exactly matched* the one that she had visualized two years prior. After an energizing interview, Sameera was offered the job and soon found herself working in her dream environment, in awe of the power of her subconscious mind.

Sometimes a visualization will astound or confound you. You will see, feel, sense, or hear something that is unexpected. You may be surprised to discover hidden interests, talents, or long-buried creative impulses. This is spontaneous visioning, when a vision arrives of its own accord.

Spontaneous or receptive visions often give you something that you didn't even *know* you needed.

When you connect with your future self while in a relaxed state, you are able to access ideas that may have been repressed in an effort to feel a sense of safety, love, or belonging. These unconscious parts have important wisdom to share. I love using guided visualization because it helps me not only manifest my current desires with greater ease (intentional visioning) but also gain clarity on what I unconsciously *really* want (spontaneous visioning). One client of mine went into a guided visualization and though she'd never thought of herself as an artist, she saw artwork and a studio. She immediately signed up for art classes, which brought her unexpected joy. Any time you receive a message or images about your desired future, write it down in your Soul Solution Journal. No detail is too small. You may be surprised as you reflect on the words you have written over the days and weeks that follow.

## How Eve Ensler's Vagina Put Me on Stage

Once, I followed my energetic bread crumbs and signed up for a feminine leadership conference called "Emerging Women." Eve Ensler, the author of *The Vagina Monologues*, was a keynote speaker, and when she took the stage, she shared a deeply personal story about being sexually abused as a child and getting diagnosed with uterine cancer as an adult.

Like Eve, my mom was sexually abused and, later in life, went through chemotherapy for ovarian cancer. As the talk ended, I leapt to my feet to join the standing ovation, tears streaming down my cheeks, and grasped the hand of the woman next to me even though we'd only just met. Eve's talk healed some old pain inside me and opened my heart in a new way. I went back to my room, stirred by the way she actively shifted people from the stage. How was that possible?

Eve's delivery opened my mind to a new idea: public speaking could be a catalyst for massive transformation. As I lay in bed that night, I visualized myself on stage. I didn't focus on what I would be talking about but rather how I wanted to *feel* and how I wanted the audience to feel. Because I had just witnessed Eve's talk, it was easy to viscerally imagine the audience responding. With the image in my mind, a lump formed in my throat. I started crying (it was a big day for crying); truth bumps ran up and down my arms.

Once home, the demands of regular life pushed the story out of my mind. Then, two weeks later, I got a call out of the blue inviting me to give a TEDx talk. I had not told a single soul about my vision of becoming a public speaker. I didn't lift a finger in networking efforts. That TEDx talk launched my whole speaking career.

It all started with honoring an energetic bread crumb and soul whisper to go to this conference, being open to receiving Eve's heart-centered message, and then harnessing the power of visualization in a moment of authentic inspiration. I felt guided by my body and my soul. The truth is, I love public speaking. I hardly get nervous before walking on stage. It's something that comes fairly easily to me, and it's like my soul knew it all along. If I had tried to reverse engineer it and decided from an ego-centric place—*I want to get paid to give keynote speeches*—it might have worked too, but it definitely would have required more exhausting effort. And it might not have felt as good.

I have had to learn this lesson (so, so, so, so) many times—not to force things, to follow my intuition, to have faith in something bigger than me. When I trust myself, trust the universe, and trust that there is a divine plan for me, things work out. I am offered the inspiration that moves me to my next step. When you use tools such as visualization, they amplify the effect of guidance. Try it for yourself and watch how things truly appear like magic.

## Visioning Circles

Over the past ten years of working with women, I've observed how much easier it is for us to see potential in others than in ourselves. A simple yet powerful way to stop playing small (as we've been culturally conditioned to do) is to participate in what I call a Visioning Circle. A Visioning Circle allows you to harness the power of a group to help everyone expand the potential vision for their life. In this safe and supportive environment, you speak your vision aloud, then other people amplify it into something even *greater* than you could imagine for yourself.

When I facilitate a Visioning Circle, one participant speaks their vision aloud, and then the others give specific feedback about when the speaker seemed most energized and clear about their vision, and when they seemed more uncertain or confused. Next, the listeners contribute their ideas and make the vision *even bigger*.

When I first began this practice, I was in the midst of a career transition, which still felt opaque. I didn't know what I wanted to do yet, which made it very hard to depict in detail. After a few visualization attempts, I switched gears and began describing my ideal home instead. My husband and I had been looking to move into a two-bedroom apartment for over a year. I saw the new home in glorious detail, mentioning everything from high ceilings and an open floor plan to natural sunlight and a bedroom for our future child. Afterward, a group member reflected, "When you talked about work, you stumbled and used lots of caveats, but when you spoke about your ideal home, wow! I could really *see* that apartment, Vanessa! It feels like home for you."

Less than three hours after speaking this vision, my husband sent me a link to an apartment on Craigslist that fit my description exactly. Within a month, we had moved in. Sometimes you may feel stuck in one area of your life, as I did with my career. As you focus on other issues, everything unfolds in natural and divine timing.

I'm convinced that one of the reasons these Visioning Circles are so powerful is because each individual's energy contributes to the collective energy of the group, which propels each individual forward. Something truly alchemical happens when you gather a group of supportive women together to call something new into their lives. It's very different from trying to do this with family or friends. Often our loved ones prefer that we stay the same because of their own unconscious needs and patterning. They aren't able to effectively hold space for a new vision of you or your life like those outside of your immediate family and social circle can.

## Segment Intending and Focusing on Your Desired Feelings

We know that setting an intention is a powerful way to clarify and align with what you want. You can do this in mini moments throughout your day with a practice called Segment Intending that I learned from the teachings of Esther and Jerry Hicks.[4] When you are transitioning from one activity to another— for example, walking down the hallway to begin your work day—pause to set an intention and visualize how you would like to *feel* during this segment of your day. Perhaps your intention is to feel focused and calm. Practice "future pacing" in which you visualize fulfilling that intention. Before sitting down at your computer, you might imagine yourself completing your top priorities with methodical ease. Before picking up the phone to make an important call, you might intend clear communication and then visualize yourself speaking with confidence. While driving to the grocery store, you may set the intention to feel relaxed and present while running errands and joyfully choose foods that will nourish your body. Observe how setting an intention paves the way for the good feelings. I recently set the intention to feel unconditional love while editing the manuscript for this book. When I call it quits for the day, I usually beat myself up with thoughts like, *You only edited two chapters, you should have done four!* But after doing Segment Intending, I noticed that my inner monologue was much more self-loving; it said, *Nice job completing two chapters!* Segment Intending is a powerful way to bring together the tools of visualization, intention setting, and shifting thought patterns. By setting a clear intention about how you want to *feel* in a specific situation, you are doing mini visioning and neural rewiring.

## Quick Soul Tip

I recommend spending several minutes each day intentionally cultivating and savoring your desired feelings. Begin by thinking of a feeling you want to experience more often—for example, peacefulness. Then imagine a time in the past when you had that feeling. Take at least three to five breaths (ideally fifteen seconds) and stay with the feeling. It can be helpful to start by remembering a past experience and then amplify and extend that feeling. At first, you'll want to quickly move on. Resist this temptation. If you want support in this practice, use the Savor the Good Guided Meditation based on the work of neuroscientist Rick Hanson[5] on my website vanessaloder.com /book to begin rewiring your brain to focus on the good.

## Take Action (Baby Steps)

Once you gain clarity on your vision, it can be useful to break it down and take a first baby step. This helps build momentum and sends a signal to the universe (and yourself!) that you're serious. Plus, creating small, doable steps is a way to mitigate perfection paralysis. Sometimes thinking about taking action can inspire fear and ultimately resistance to your vision. In these instances, forget about the vision until the next step arrives, as I did with keynote speaking, or when you're in a more receptive mood. Part of The Soul Solution is tuning in to your own intuition about which approach best serves you in a given situation.

Another simple and powerful action you can take to make your vision more concrete is to make a soul board—a purely intuitive, nonverbal creative exercise that will help you reconnect with your unconscious desires. As you may recall, the soul expresses itself in pictures, symbols, and feelings. Create your soul board by cutting out images (that represent your goals and desires) that feel good to you and putting them into a unique collage. At first blush, this might look like a silly craft project, but it goes much deeper than that.

Yanelle, a client who is a left-brained engineer, shared, "Vanessa, when you first suggested I make a soul board, I thought, *This is silly!* Then, halfway through, I saw this gorgeous painting of a farmhouse from a discarded art calendar and **knew** I had to put an offer on that home in the country. It was so bizarre, but you were right."

Now that you have learned about the power of visualization, you have the tools to unlock a bolder and more soul-centric vision for your life. You also have ways to begin feeling a greater sense of satisfaction with all that you've already accomplished, and you understand how to manifest success without all the hustle by leveraging the power of your subconscious mind. (Yay you!) Keep attuning to yourself and carving out the time and space to stay focused on what really matters!

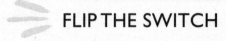

# FLIP THE SWITCH

## Creating Your Soul Board

Supplies:

- Poster board or large piece of paper
- A handful of different magazines
- Double-sided tape
- Markers or pens
- A few photos of yourself

Instructions:

1. Listen to the Future Self Guided Visualization on my website vanessaloder.com/book.

2. Have fun pulling out images, words, or quotes that you like from the magazines.

3. Cut out anything that resonates with you and makes you feel good: pictures that symbolize the experiences, feelings, and objects you want to attract into your life. Don't judge! Instead, listen to your intuition when an image resonates with you. Ask, *What does my heart want? What is my soul telling me?* You may be surprised by what attracts your attention in this phase.

4. When you feel ready, begin to lay out your favorite images on the board however you like. Let your intuition guide you. It can be helpful to create sections for work, love, play, family, and so forth. It's fine to have cutout words on your board such as *joy* or *ignite*, and I recommend including at least three or more **images** to inspire your subconscious and evoke a more emotional response. Choose the images that trigger the strongest feelings in your body.

5. Discard any images or words that don't feel right, remembering there is beauty in simplicity and clarity.

6. Stick your images onto your board using the double-sided tape.

7. If you feel inclined, add handwritten words and personalize your board even further by adding joyful photos of yourself. You can put your face on the cover of a magazine or insert a photo of you next to someone you'd like to work with or meet.

8. Take a photo of your soul board with your phone and look at it every night before bed. You can even make it your screen saver so it continually pops up.

9. Place your board somewhere in your home or office where you'll see it often.

10. Dance it out! Play music that energizes you while dancing in front of your soul board and soaking in the images. Bonus points if you get goose bumps or tingly, exhilarating sensations while doing this.

## Ten Things Tool

This is one of the fastest ways to feel better about everything you are *already* doing and encourage an appreciation mindset, which creates positive forward momentum toward your goals.

In your Soul Solution Journal, make a list of ten things to celebrate and appreciate that you did last week. If you're feeling frustrated at work or undervalued as a caregiver, for instance, focus the list on that. I often add both personal and professional elements to my list, and I always include things that I care about but that no one pats me on the back for doing—such as making sure my kids eat healthy food. You may need to look at your calendar to remember what you did last week—from being patient with your kids to speaking up at work. Even if you can't think of ten things easily, keep going! At the end of this activity, you'll be amazed at all you do!

# Write Your Movie Script

Set aside at least twenty to forty minutes to do this activity. Imagine you're a screenwriter writing a movie whose protagonist is *you*. The movie is about you living your dream life. You are the writer, director, and producer of this movie.

1. Get out your Soul Solution Journal and complete the previous Ten Things Tool to get your appreciation juices flowing.

2. Spend a few minutes connecting with your heart. You can use the Heart Wisdom and the Five-Foot Bubble guided meditation from chapter 1 at vanessaloder.com/book, or simply spend three to five minutes with one or both hands on your heart as you connect with your breath.

3. Choose a timeline for your vision. I recommend five or ten years in the future, but if you want to focus on a near-term project or goal, you may choose a shorter timeline, such as six or twelve months.

4. Set a timer for a minimum of twenty minutes. Write your movie script in stream-of-consciousness, "hot pen" style (the pen never leaves the page).

5. Go big. Allow yourself to be delighted by what emerges. Make it extraordinary. Include something wild or random. Describe the most inspiring life. Don't worry about being practical. Write from your heart.

6. Write in the third-person present tense about yourself. Imagine a scene from a movie, then describe it: "Sameera is walking down the street to her new office building with a spring in her step. She can't believe how lucky she is to work with this brilliant, kindhearted group of people."

7. Write quickly. Don't pause to judge, edit, or reread as you go.

8. Finish your first draft. Take a break. Go outside, stretch, go to sleep.

9. Revisit what you wrote after a day or week. Revise the movie script however you want. Add new scenes, delete old ones. Remember, you have *complete* creative control.

10. Reread your final script. Notice how it makes you *feel*. If it doesn't excite you (and possibly frighten you a bit), revise to improve and make it even more expansive. Remember, our greatest fear often lies next to our greatest desire.[6]

## Soul Symbol

## Kan
(pronounced kan)

This symbol represents creation and manifestation. Now is the time to plant the seed of a new intention, dream, or project. All seeds are holographic and designed to grow into their own wholeness, as are you. Breathe in and out deeply while gazing at this symbol and ask yourself, *What inspiration, project, dream, or intention wants to be seeded and initiated at this time?*

My dreams contain an intrinsic knowing and the power of their own completion.

I say yes to seeding my heart's desire.

*Chapter 7*

# RADICAL
# RESPONSIBILITY

**M**any years ago, my boyfriend (now husband), Brent, and I were walking down the uneven, cobblestone streets in Medford, Oregon, licking ice-cream cones in the dappled afternoon sunlight, when we stumbled upon a jewelry store. Brent playfully nudged my shoulder and suggested we pop in to get my ring finger sized. I froze. Panic welled up in my chest and throat as I mumbled excuses: "We're on vacation! It's inconvenient. I want to personally know the jeweler." The happy moment deflated like a balloon pierced with a BB gun. We fell into a tense silence as our abandoned ice cream dripped down our hands. After three years of dating, Brent was eager to get engaged. He'd started dropping hints, which left me feeling pressured and uncomfortable. I thought after living together for a year I'd feel readier to get married. Instead, I was scared to death.

I felt guilty knowing so many other girls who were eager to get engaged. I kept hoping my feelings would change. So, after the ring-store debacle, I took a long, hard look at my relationship. Was I scared because I didn't want to marry this guy? No. It wasn't actually about him or even us. It was about *me*. After witnessing my parents' ugly divorce, I had a lot of fear about marriage. This was a pivotal moment when I started facing my own shadow.

I began learning what it means to take radical responsibility for your own side of the street. I made a commitment to seek support and hired an executive coach who had changed my friend's life for the better. She would change my life too.

The coach taught me what it means to take responsibility for my feelings, stories, and choices. When I had negative thoughts about marriage, she had me practice mindfulness, consciously labeling the negative thought "the voice of fear" and taking deep breaths while noticing the physical sensations in my body until they dissipated. I would also ask myself, *When have I felt these feelings before?* Often, childhood memories would surface, along with shame, anger, sadness, and everything in between. It was incredibly uncomfortable at times, but it was worth it. A year later, I felt ready to get engaged.

## What Is Radical Responsibility?

After coming into awareness of your current unhappiness or dissatisfaction and beginning to tune in to your deeper truth, radical responsibility is the next step. Radical responsibility is when you decide to take 100 percent responsibility for your life. As I learned from the work of the personal growth pioneers Katie and Gay Hendricks, many of us exist in victim mode, feeling like we're at the whim of others, external events, or even the political system. Others get stuck in hero or savior mode, taking too much responsibility and trying to fix other people's problems. Still others go into villain mode, blaming and criticizing rather than taking responsibility for contributing to the situation.

Radical responsibility is the precursor to any inner change, founded on the fundamental premise that we alone have the power to change our situations. Otherwise, we risk staying stuck, as if we're victims of circumstances beyond our control.

## Do You Shirk Responsibility?

Ever have a bad day, when it feels like everyone else is a problem and then you realize that the only common denominator is you? Many of us place blame or focus elsewhere to our own detriment without even realizing it. Katie and Gay Hendricks developed a "triangle" framework for the victim, hero, and villain roles to help determine if you're shirking responsibility, with questions such as "Are you trying to find blame with yourself or others; are you seeking a scapegoat (villain position)?" and "Are you claiming a victim role by feeling overwhelmed, powerless, and waiting for someone else to fix the problem (victim position)?"[1] When you're in villain mode, you're often focused on a single right answer, blaming others (or yourself). Villains tend to stifle open discussion or creative problem-solving; as the villain, you shirk responsibility by blaming others or yourself in a way that's counterproductive. Victims, on the other hand, avoid responsibility by complaining, worrying, acting like martyrs, and assuming a powerless position. Heroes often swoop in to fix and solve everyone's problems, trying to control or change the situation in order to avoid feeling pain or discomfort. Often we combine the hero, victim, and villain roles. For example, I often play the hero role by picking up my kids' dirty socks and loading the dishwasher (*I've got this!*), then I go into a martyr position (*Why is it all put on me?*), and occasionally follow up with a good dose of villain energy (*Shape up or ship out!*).

## The Heroine Trap

If you're a type-A woman, chances are you're a competent problem-solver who tends to take on more than 100 percent of the responsibility, falling into a hero role. It's faster and easier for you to just do things yourself, so you do. Plus, it can feel good to be needed. But if you're always the go-to person, you leave no space to *go to* your own source, focus on what really matters, and fill your own well.

If this rings true, it may mean that, for you, taking responsibility involves **not helping others**. This is a radical concept for driven women. On the surface, this may look like doing *less*, but it will be one of the hardest things you ever do. Not taking on everyone else's burdens is an act of empowerment for many women. The next time someone comes to you with a problem or an extra project, ask yourself, *Why am I taking this on, and how does it serve my values and bigger why?* After learning about radical responsibility, one of my past clients used this expression to stop herself from taking on too much: "Not my circus, not my monkeys."

## Radical Responsibility in Four Steps

Taking radical responsibility becomes easier with these four questions from Katie and Gay Hendricks, taught to me by executive coach Alex Merrin. Here's how it works:

### Step 1: What Is My Primary Complaint?
*Choose a Complaint, Complain for Two Full Minutes*

Think of something in your life that's going poorly—work, relationships, health, finances, anything that feels alive for you today. This first time, choose something bothersome but not traumatic or extreme—for example, coworkers who aren't completing their portion of a shared task.

Once you've chosen your situation, put two minutes on a clock and begin complaining—aloud by yourself, with a partner, or on paper. You must complain for the full two minutes. Don't censor yourself. Don't try to be aware of your own stuff. Go into full whining and blaming mode. This is your chance to finally get it all out!

When the two minutes are up, *pause*. Notice how you *feel* in your body.

Do you notice a rush of energy? Do you feel a bit high? Most people get a hit of adrenaline from complaining. There's an actual **chemical payoff**, which is why it's addictive though rarely productive.

Some people also notice that after complaining for two full minutes, the issue doesn't seem that big a deal anymore. Continue the exercise regardless.

### Step 2: How Am I Contributing to This Situation?

Next, ask yourself, *Hmmm, how am I contributing to this situation?* Answer aloud or in your Soul Solution Journal for two full minutes. Though it might feel silly, according to Katie and Gay, it can help to make the noise *Hmmm* aloud as this connects you with your brain's creative side. I've found this to be true in my experience and that of my clients, so give it a shot even if it seems weird.

This is the step where you begin to take responsibility, and it will feel uncomfortable. You may want to distract yourself or make excuses. Keep going.

Be really honest. For example, "I haven't told my coworkers how I feel about taking on so much of the workload." Or "I don't trust the quality of their work and tend to micromanage."

If you do this with a partner, neither of you should respond. Simply practice mindful listening. You'll likely want to reassure the person speaking, offering advice or commiseration. Please don't. Simply be present with yourself and the person speaking by noticing the rise and fall of your chest or belly as you breathe.

You may struggle with the question, but there's always an answer. Perhaps you're staying at a job or in a relationship that makes you miserable. Staying can be one way you're contributing to a negative situation.

Most people initially feel resistance and shame when they begin taking responsibility, followed by elation and empowerment as they realize they have more agency than they initially thought. So, if you feel crappy during step 2, that's normal. But it's worth it. On the other side of those uncomfortable feelings lies your true power to get what you want in life.

### Step 3: What Would I *Really* Like?

The tricky part about step 3 is that you must answer *What would I really like?* with something that's in *your* control and can be initiated by *you*. Usually what you would like is for the jackass you are complaining about to change their horrible behavior. But you can only take responsibility for your side of the street.

One example I like to give for this step involves my wonderful husband again. He has this lovely habit of lightly rinsing dirty dishes, then stacking them on the counter near the dishwasher. This used to really irritate me. I would think, *You're 80 percent there; just load the dang dishwasher!* For step 3, I might be tempted to say, "What I really want is for my husband to finish the damn job!" But do I have control over that? No.

Sometimes when you're asking *What do I really want?* you need to take things to a more macro level. In the example above, what I *really* want is to have a clean kitchen without clutter. Now that I've expanded what I want, suddenly I have more room for new and creative solutions: I could hire someone to clean our house. We could ask the babysitter to help load the dishwasher. We could encourage the kids to help clean areas of visual clutter in the house, and so forth. The solution is not solely dependent on my husband changing his behavior in one small and specific way.

Whether at work or at home, often what we *really* want on a deeper level is to feel appreciated. For instance, if your husband isn't going to finish the dishes, it would be nice if he said thank you when you did it! We can show this appreciation to ourselves or even request it of others. While we can't control whether they're willing to say yes, we can communicate how much it means to us.

### Step 4: What Am I Willing to Do to Create That?

The next step is to ask yourself, *What am I willing to do to create that?* But before you do, say *Hmmm* aloud to get your creative juices flowing. Spend one to two minutes speaking your answer aloud to yourself or a partner, or writing it down in your Soul Solution Journal. It's important to keep answering the question for at least one full minute as you may be surprised by what comes out toward the end.

Once you have an idea of what you are willing to do, distill it down to a simple action step that you can do in the next week.

For example: "I will schedule a meeting with my team leader by 4 p.m. on Thursday to tell him I've been feeling resentful about taking on too much of this project, even though I initially volunteered. I will acknowledge that I tend to take on too much and ask for his support in helping me change this pattern of taking more than 100 percent responsibility for everyone else's work."

## Quick Soul Tip

The next time you notice yourself complaining about something or *someone*, answer these questions based on the work of Gay and Katie Hendricks:

1. How am I contributing to this situation?
2. What is it I really want (that's in my control and can be initiated by me)?
3. What am I willing to do to create that?

When circumstances feel out of your control, remember that while you cannot control the events or people around you, you do have control over your response in any given situation. Take two to three breaths and choose a response that feels better.

When I first sought help to deal with my fear of marriage, I felt so much shame. My boyfriend's parents were happily married, while my parents were divorced, and my family was complicated. One of my deepest fears was that I was damaged goods, and he was not. When I looked at the reality of my trepidation to get married compared to my boyfriend's enthusiasm, it was hard not to feel crappy about myself. But I still looked at that uncomfortable truth and then made a commitment to reach out and get support. That is when things started to change for the better for me.

Taking responsibility is essential to finding The Soul Solution. You cannot live from your core self, or soul, when you are blaming or fixing others. In order to take radical responsibility and clean up your side of the street, you have to be *aware* of your own response or behavior in a given situation. This is where mindfulness comes in.

## The Power of Mindfulness (E + R = O)

Mindfulness is probably the single most helpful tool when it comes to recognizing, but not judging, our own radical responsibility. Years ago, Jack Kornfield, a Buddhist teacher and the founder of Spirit Rock Meditation Center, told me a story about a war veteran who, due to anger management issues, was referred to an eight-week mindfulness training course. Several weeks into the program, the man was at the grocery store early in the evening, hangry for dinner. Waiting in line at the checkout with a cart full of groceries, he felt impatient. In line ahead of him was a woman in her sixties holding a baby. She was moving slowly and had a single can of soup in her cart.

Things only got worse from there: The clerk began to coo over the infant and even held the child in her arms at one point. The veteran threw his hands up out of frustration and was about to explode at all involved when he remembered his mindfulness training. He had a split second of self-awareness in which he observed and labeled his emotion: *Oh, anger.*

He took two deep, slow breaths. By the time he finished, the woman and baby were leaving the store. Now calm, the veteran turned to the clerk and said, "That was a cute baby."

"Aw, you think?" she smiled. "Thank you so much. That's my son. My husband was killed in the war. I had to take this job to make ends meet, and I don't get to see my baby as much as I'd like. My mom brings my son in every day during my shift so I can see him." The soldier began openly crying in the middle of the checkout lane. He hadn't realized how much his anger and judgment had prevented him from feeling the compassion and love that was always available to him. He left a changed person.

This story never fails to touch my heart. What I love most about it, aside from the raw humanity and love, is how it demonstrates the power of mindfulness to allow us to slow down and take responsibility for our response in any given situation.

As it turns out, we can't access the things we crave most deeply, such as love and belonging, if we aren't present in the moment. This is why mindfulness can be so life-changing.

## Taking Responsibility for Your Response

Jack Canfield, the bestselling author and motivational coach, came up with the equation:

$$E + R = O$$
Event + Response = Outcome[2]

We often don't have control over the events in our lives, but we *always* have control over whether we react out of love or fear in a given situation. **Our response is where our power lies.**

As author Stephen R. Covey is credited for saying, "Between stimulus and response there is a space. In that space is our power to choose our response. In our response lies our growth and our freedom."[3] Practicing mindfulness helps you create this S P A C E, allowing you to take responsibility for your reactions in the moment.

Events + (Mindful Pause) + Healthier
Response = Better Outcomes

Neuroscientists once believed the brain becomes static when we reach adulthood, but we actually create new neural pathways all the time. One study of London taxi drivers showed their brains' hippocampi grew and their memories improved as a result of memorizing twenty-five thousand streets.[4]

Thanks to this neuroplasticity, the more we practice more positive reactions, the more they come naturally. As the neuropsychologist Donald O. Hebb said, "Neurons that fire together, wire together."

Imagine the very first time you were stuck in traffic. At first that annoyance may have been mild and came slowly. Over time, a well-trodden pathway develops between traffic and anger in your brain. Eventually you have a five-lane neural superhighway in your brain that is so ingrained it becomes automatic. Maybe you even start to feel triggered before you turn on your car.

The good news is that if we take radical responsibility for our choices, we can close down habitual negative roadways and build new positive neural pathways to appreciation, joy, and calm. Each time we make the effort to focus on the positive and on our own accountability, we're literally paving the way for more positivity down the road. How cool is that?! As an overachiever, it's easy to love this concept because it means that all our hard inner work is going to pay off in spades . . . well, in new neural pathways, to be exact.

## The Downward Spiral

Have you ever said something in a meeting and instantly regretted it? Then, minutes later, you thought of the brilliant thing you wish you'd said?

If you're like me (and most people), you end up spending the rest of the day ruminating on what happened and berating yourself on replay. You imagine how other people reacted, the looks on their faces, what you should have said instead. Your inner critic has a field day.

Here's the interesting part: your body can't tell the difference between the *imagined* scenario and the *real* one. So, on a physiological level, every time you relive the stressful event in your mind, your body releases adrenaline and the stress hormone cortisol. It's exhausting and depleting.

After beating yourself up all afternoon, you finally leave work and head home, but you're still stewing as you walk in the door to your house. You're eagerly greeted by a loved one (a partner, child, or pet), but you're short, distant, and distracted. You snap at them. They recoil. So, you get into a big fight. Next thing you know, dinner is ruined.

Sometimes in these types of scenarios, I even notice that I'm picking a fight, but I can't seem to stop myself. This is the downward spiral—when a single bad event creates a negative domino effect. It's the pits.

The good news is that with E + R = O, you can interrupt this pattern of negativity and start to practice radical responsibility. It may feel forced, but if you pause and take two or three deep breaths or remember three things you're grateful for, you will start to **interrupt the negative cycle** and you'll be back on track.

Just naming it can begin to quell its power over you: *Oh, I'm in a downward spiral.* Like the veteran in the grocery store, this awareness pops you out of *being* the emotion and into the seat of the observer. Suddenly you have a higher level of consciousness about what you're experiencing. It's so powerful to notice your patterns.

**Awareness** occurs in the moment when you recognize you're in a downward spiral and you name your painful truth. **Radical responsibility** is the moment immediately after, when you choose to do something to change your situation or mind-state.

## Make a Commitment

Even with awareness, change is not easy. Anyone who has ever accomplished anything lasting experiences fear at the onset. But if you are *truly* committed to achieving something, then the universe will conspire to provide it for you.

Have you ever had an experience where things just seemed to work out in your favor? When you make a big commitment to create something in your life and trust the process, outside forces inexplicably come to your aid. Miracles happen.

How do you become truly committed?

One important step in taking radical responsibility is to commit to building the life you want. Making a "Commitment Statement," a process I also learned from Katie and Gay Hendricks, is a powerful way to set a clear and conscious intention.[5] It will also support you in moving through fear, resistance, and shame, which you're bound to encounter as you examine your responsibility on your Soul Solution journey.

# FLIP THE SWITCH

## The Victim, Villain, or Hero Quiz

This exercise is based on the work of Katie and Gay Hendricks.[6] Think of a challenging situation or a relationship struggle you're facing right now. Then read these phrases aloud and note which ones resonate the most:

A. "I've got this."

B. "There's nothing I can do."

C. "Who's to blame?"

A. "I can handle it."

B. "I have to."

C. "It should be different."

A. "I can help."

B. "It's hard."

C. "You're wrong."

Count up your letters. Mostly A's is the *hero* pattern, mostly B's is the *victim* pattern, and mostly C's is the *villain* pattern. We all embody each of these, but we often have a main default. Are you taking too little or too much responsibility?

Next, shift back to radical responsibility by answering the four questions from earlier:

1. What is my complaint?

2. How am I contributing to the situation?

3. What would I *really* like?

4. What am I willing to do to create that?

Take three deep breaths and repeat, "I take 100 percent responsibility, no more, no less. I am exactly where I need to be.

Other people are where they are. Other people's suffering and happiness depends on their thoughts and actions, not my wishes for them."

## How to Create a Commitment Statement

According to Katie and Gay Hendricks, a good Commitment Statement should be:

- Positive

- Present tense

- Include a juicy action verb (*savoring, discovering, celebrating, loving*)[7]

Start with the words "I commit to . . ." and put yourself in the middle of the action. For example, "I commit to exploring my creativity and discovering meaningful work" is more powerful than "I commit to becoming creative." The word *becoming* implies you're not doing it yet.

For inspiration, here are some sample career-related statements:

- I commit to creating work I love.

- I commit to following my heart and intuition for six months to create work I love.

- I commit to launching a new business that is profitable with ease.

- I commit to discovering my full creative expression and inspiring others to find theirs.

- I commit to learning from my mistakes and using them for inspiration.

This is my favorite all-inclusive Commitment Statement inspired by *The Big Leap*:[8]

"I commit to expanding in love, abundance, joy, creativity, and ease every single day, and inspiring those around me to do the same."

As you're making this new commitment, don't worry about *how* it will unfold. The how will reveal itself one step at a time.

The reason many people avoid making commitments is because they first want a **guarantee**. Unfortunately that's not how it works. Imagine you wanted to learn how to swim, and you studied books and videos but refused to get into the pool until you were guaranteed to float. You'd never make real progress!

Once you've chosen your personal Commitment Statement, it will become your mantra for the next several months. Write it on an index card or sticky note to keep on your nightstand. Don't forget to read your Commitment Statement each night before bed and again when you wake up.

## Embody Your Commitment

Take at least ten to fifteen minutes for this exercise, perhaps when you first wake up. Read your Commitment Statement aloud two to three times. Then do one of the activities below for five to ten minutes to raise your vibration:

- Find a quiet space to sit in silence and meditate or take three to six deep breaths.

- Walk in nature.

- Take a bath.

- Dance to fun music.

- Lie on the floor and listen to music that relaxes you and brings you joy.

After you've completed the activity and noticed your energy rise, repeat your statement one more time and ask yourself aloud, "Hmmm, what is one action I can take **today** to move toward this commitment?"

See if you can allow the answer to bubble up from inside rather than forcing it. Having put yourself in a relaxed or high vibrational state, you may be surprised by the answer you receive.

## Take Action

It's very important that you take action on your Commitment Statement *today*, even if it's a very small step. Write that action down with a self-imposed deadline.

## Recommit

We're only human. We all slip up now and again. Equally important to making this commitment is your ability to *recommit* when things don't go as planned. When you slip up, repeat your Commitment Statement and create a new action step.

It's okay to create a new Commitment Statement anytime you want to or to have more than one in play. However, I recommend starting with just one for the first couple of weeks.

Whenever you make a commitment, you're telling the universe that you're ready for something different and taking the first step toward creating that new reality. Let your commitment lead. You can't go wrong.

## Soul Symbol

### Lamat
(pronounced la-mat')

This symbol opens the aperture and helps you expand your perspective to access greater harmony with your True Self. Gazing at this symbol, notice your field of vision extend as you invite in a simultaneous awareness of the desires of the ego self and the wisdom of the True Self. Breathe in and out deeply while gazing at this symbol and say to yourself, *I step back from my small-minded perspective to access the self-acceptance and harmony that comes with an expanded focus.*

I expand my perception of truth.

I say yes to all of me.

*Chapter 8*

# QUIETING YOUR INNER CRITIC

magine a two-year-old child with chunky little thighs and chocolate smeared across her face running gleefully toward the playground. She giggles with delight as she crawls through the tunnel of a play structure. When she comes out the other side, another child throws sand in her hair. She begins to wail at this sudden assault on her joy.

What's that toddler's inner dialogue as she cries? She's upset, of course, until a parent comforts her and sends her back off to play. What she's not doing is criticizing or blaming herself. She's not thinking, *Look at me, I'm a mess! My thighs are huge! I shouldn't have eaten so many brownies. I probably looked silly crawling through the tunnel. No wonder that kid threw sand at me! Maybe if I clean up my face, people will be nicer to me tomorrow.*

That would seem ludicrous, right? Yet we talk to ourselves in this harsh manner every single day.

We come into this world with an intrinsic belief in our own worthiness and beauty. We don't question it. Then as we get older, the adults around us praise us when we excel in ways they deem important and offer veiled (or unbridled) judgment when we don't meet expectations. They don't believe *they* are enough and so they tell us *we* aren't enough, which creates this never-ending not-enoughness loop. It's natural that we start to wonder, *Am I enough?* This self-doubt lodges itself in the back of our psyche and manifests as self-criticism compounded by media, advertising, social media, and more. As women in the modern world, we're inundated with negative messaging: we're too fat, too ugly, too loud, too quiet, too needy, too selfish, too old, too young, too much, too little. It's almost impossible not to internalize these external messages about our flaws—until we start waking up. To exorcise this negativity, we have to identify the voices inside our heads, transforming our private drill sergeants into compassionate inner allies. We can remind ourselves, *I'm doing the best I can. Other people struggle with this too. I'm not alone. It's going to be okay. May I be kind to myself in this moment.* Phew, I can feel my nervous system relaxing just reading those words.

If you pay attention, you'll notice that the voices inside your head aren't just dishing out harsh criticism of yourself and others. They're commenting on your entire existence: *Oh, look, a blue VW Bug. That reminds me of my ex-boyfriend's car. He isn't still dating Sheila, is he?!* Your inner voices have something to say about *everything.*

One December morning, while we were eating our breakfast of Eggs McLoder (my husband's invention) and listening to Christmas carols, my daughter Eva asked, "Mommy, what's your book about?" I told her one of the chapters was about "making the voices in our heads speak more nicely to us." She wanted to understand more.

"We all have voices in our heads that talk to us constantly," I explained. "They say things like, 'Did you remember to water the plants? Have you texted Gemma's mom about that playdate? You want to write a book. Do you really have the time for that? I'm not sure you're the best writer. Oh, Christmas carols! FA LA LA LA LA, LA LA LA LA.'"

When I started shout-singing the last part like a crazy person, Eva started cracking up. But it was when I compared being inside my own head to living with a really annoying roommate who never stops talking that Eva totally grasped the concept.

Have you paused to listen to your inner roommate lately? It's nutso. As the novelist and activist Anne Lamott says, "My mind is a neighborhood I try not to go into alone."[1]

The voices inside our heads often say horrible things that if we heard said aloud, we'd reject immediately. As you begin to externalize these voices and get to know the many parts of your psyche, you'll learn to soften your inner dialogue.

In addition to your inner critic, lots of other voices compete for airtime in your head: the inner dictator, the inner taskmaster, the inner fearmonger, the inner protector, the inner caroler or singer, the inner skeptic, the voice of reason, and so forth. None of these voices come from your soul. They're not part of your true essence, which is a nameless, wordless presence grounded in a profound sense of awareness.

You can create a separation from those harsh inner voices when you pause to step back and really listen. In the role of observer, you create distance between your True Self and the chatter. You step into the seat of awareness—awareness of awareness itself. This may sound abstract, but take a few moments today to notice your inner talk and then ask yourself, *Who is observing these voices?*

Aside from stepping into the seat of the observer, how else can I soften or create distance from these inner voices?

Many years ago, I went on a retreat where we meditated from six in the morning to nine at night. When they rang the gong each evening, I was thankful to be done for the day. But as I left the meditation hall one day, I noticed people who opted to stay even longer. My inner judge thought, *Are they trying to get* extra credit? *These people are nuts!* Underneath that criticism lay my own insecurity and competitive nature wondering if I was doing it right and wanting to be the best. Even with meditation, I felt envious of others who might be "better" at it.

A few nights later, I was able to shift my negative thoughts about myself and the others as our teacher led us in a loving-kindness practice with various ways to practice self-compassion. My heart felt open and full in a way I hadn't experienced in years. Waves of love washed over me as I lay in the dark, tears streaming down my face. It felt incredible.

When the teacher ended the practice, I didn't want those good feelings to stop. So I stayed. I became one of *those* people. With my heart wide open in love, I laughed at myself and all my judgments and insecurities. When my practice felt complete, I folded my soft green blanket and laid it on my meditation bench, knowing it would be waiting for me at six o'clock the next morning. I gathered up my slippers and quietly left the hall feeling elated, calm, and deeply in love with myself and all of life. As I padded back to my room under the bright night stars and silvery moonlight, a single question surfaced in my mind: *How can I have more of this?*

Over the coming years, I began to notice my inner dialogue and to slowly separate myself from it. I learned how to have my own back instead of tearing myself to shreds. And this has made all the difference in my ability to take risks, overcome failure and shame, stay resilient in the face of adversity, and feel more joy and compassion.

## Ugly Roadside Trash Can Lead to Self-Love

A unique process I developed that leverages the concept of neuroplasticity to help you cultivate acceptance and joy is to practice stretching your appreciation muscles on inanimate objects you normally judge harshly. For example, while on a run or driving, look at the beautiful scenery around you and feel a true sense of savoring the light filtering through the leaves of an oak tree or the bright orange colors of fall. Then see if you can apply this same appreciation to a piece of trash on the side of the road or to the bright orange of a traffic cone. If you can cultivate appreciation toward inanimate objects you feel neutral or negative toward, you'll strengthen those neural pathways. This will make it easier for you to feel appreciation regardless of the people or circumstances around you.

There is a loop on a dirt path next to a bike trail that I run once or twice a week in our neighborhood. I often use this time running to practice various mindfulness and energy-enhancing techniques because it feels like my runner's high amplifies the impact of these capabilities. I'll start my run with a clear intention, such as *I want to feel really good while on this run and be fully present in my body, noticing and observing things with all five senses and appreciating the beauty and nature all around me.*

Lately I have combined saying loving-kindness phrases with being fully present in my environment. So, after doing some cycles of breathing to get myself present in the moment with all five senses, I will look at a beautiful, gnarled old oak tree and say in my mind, *I love you.* Then I'll turn my focus to a pretty purple flower and think, *I love you.* One day, I was running on my usual path when I noticed this rusty post with bright orange plastic netting that had fallen over at an awkward angle into the foliage. It looked so fake, unnatural, and trashy in the middle of these gorgeous woods. I thought, *Ugh, that's so ugly. Someone should clean it up.* It distracted me from the practice of being present and saying *I love you* to all the beautiful nature around me. The discarded plastic netting felt like an affront to my heightened senses as I was blissfully appreciating nature and feeling so deeply connected to all that is. I was annoyed by it. It was impeding *my* experience.

Now each time I run by the orange netting on my loop, I look toward it and think, *I love you.* At first, it felt awkward and forced. The orange netting didn't belong there in nature among all that beauty. Yet what if I saw it as beautiful too?

Something strange began to happen as I continued running my loop and thinking *I love you* each time I passed the orange netting. A fondness grew in me for the orange netting, until it became a regular and joyful part of my run. I would eagerly anticipate the moment when it came into view, straining my neck a little as I approached the turn to make sure it was still there. I was astonished at my change of heart. And the truth is, if someone from the Park Service finally did come and clean up that orange netting, I would feel a sense of loss. It seems bizarre, but it's true. And while it may sound like a leap to say that loving orange netting has helped me love the parts of myself and others I don't like, I feel in my bones this is true.

Experiment with this practice for yourself. Begin stretching your appreciation muscles toward something you deem "ugly" that you pass by on a regular basis while in your car or on a walk or a run. Begin saying and thinking *I love you* or *You're beautiful* each time you pass by that "hideous" thing. Simply observe yourself, notice your resistance or your reaction each time you attempt to give love or appreciation for this inanimate object or dirty, unseemly thing. See if your heart begins to change, and as it does, imagine how you are growing new neural pathways in your brain to help you be more accepting, compassionate, and loving toward people, objects, and situations that may not initially inspire kindness in you. Beginning to accept the things you cannot change and taking action to change the things you can are both forms of radical responsibility.

The strategies for confronting these issues really work, but you must work the tools to get the most benefit. If you've been hard on yourself your entire life, you may not cultivate a kind, gentle, compassionate voice overnight, and that's okay. It takes dedicated, consistent practice to access this new voice. There's not necessarily a singular dramatic moment when you find The Soul Solution with your internal dialogue. It's about the dozens of small choices you make each day to turn away from the negative or vapid self-chatter and focus on something that feels better. The good news is your investment in building these inner muscles will pay off, and you *will* start hearing a new, kinder, gentler voice. And when the old voice begins to dominate, you'll be able to redirect your attention quicker, knowing that the inner critic isn't synonymous with you.

## The Voice That Lies

One night after feeling tired all week, I decided I would finally catch up on sleep. I got all cozy under my comforter, clean crisp sheets, and favorite velvety blanket, and was finally drifting off when our four-year-old son started yelling, "Mommy, Daddy, MOMMY!" With a glance at my husband, who snored away with his earplugs and eye mask, I sighed, rose, and went to investigate. It turned out that my son's nightlight had simply gotten unplugged, so after delivering some kisses on his soft little cheeks, I returned to bed, affirming to myself, *This little disruption won't bother me at all. I can fall right back asleep with ease.* Only I didn't.

Two hours later I was still wide awake and frustrated, so I decided to read a book. When I turned off my light again around 2 a.m., my mind began spinning stories about how *awful* I was going to feel the next day.

Have you ever had a similar experience? The mindfulness teacher Tara Brach often talks about "the second arrow," based on a Buddhist parable about how to approach suffering.[2]

Let's say you really lose your patience and yell at your kid. That's the first arrow. Many of us might spend hours or even days afterward beating ourselves up, thinking, *Why did I do that? I'm the worst parent.*

The second arrow lands when our mind starts weaving stories about how awful things are, which usually causes us more suffering than the first. When we start to pay attention, we often notice that the actual moment of pain or difficulty isn't as bad as the story we tell ourselves *about it afterward*.

Your mind's tendency to get stuck in unhelpful loops is why mindfulness and meditation are so useful. If you can take that moment of pause between the event and your response (remember: Event + Response = Outcome), you have a shot at experiencing the first arrow but then noticing your inner dialogue and dodging the second one.

> There is a Buddhist saying: pain is
> inevitable, suffering is optional.

If I'm being honest about my own experience and the experiences of the hundreds of women I've supported, I'd guess that we are shooting in the range of seventeen to thirty-seven arrows after the first arrow. I just made that up, but it feels about right. We're repeating each painful story or self-criticism over and over again to the point where it becomes our way of thinking and magnifies our suffering. We need to get out of our own way in order to hear our soul whispers and follow through in pursuit of our True North Star.

## Stop Shooting the Second Arrow

Your mission, should you choose to accept it, is to notice the volley of arrows you're launching at yourself and then . . . stop shooting! Whether you catch yourself at the eleventh or thirty-seventh arrow doesn't matter, whether it's the minute after you begin or three days later. Instead of continuing to launch arrows, pay attention to your breath. Notice the colors in the room. Practice self-compassion (see this chapter's "Flip the Switch" exercises). Call a friend. Listen to music. Do anything to stop skewering yourself.

## Quick Soul Tip

The next time you're being hard on yourself, playfully say to yourself this phrase adapted from Jen Sincero's book *You Are a Badass*: *I'm just a little bunny doing my best*. It sounds silly, but give it a try, it really helps!

Or, imagine a good friend of yours in that same situation. What would you say to that person? Then envision that friend offering those same kind words to you.

## Frumpy and Friendless

The other morning, I was headed back to my car after my son's preschool drop-off when I noticed two moms—one of whom I know and think is cool—talking in a huddle. I approached and said hello, then stood awkwardly outside their two-person circle as they continued their conversation without me. They both looked polished and groomed. I was in gray sweats with a big stain on the chest and a puffy vest I've never liked. My hair was not brushed.

After what felt like eons of awkwardness, I said goodbye and left. Before I had even pulled out of the parking lot, I began berating myself: *You have no cute clothes. You haven't made any close friends in the East Bay. When was the last time you washed your hair?* But then a miracle occurred. I channeled The Soul Solution! In the midst of listening to and believing my inner critic, I caught myself . . . and I stopped. Take that, arrow!

I started intentionally noticing the beautiful surrounding nature—dappled sunlight streaming through the branches, countless shades of green. It worked! For a minute. But then the voice returned with a vengeance, insisting I should *definitely* go shopping and get cuter clothes. Maybe that chic yoga brand? New sneakers? Though I caught myself again, it was trickier to recognize the voice this time because it wasn't being overtly critical so much as "helpful." The voice inside your head can be very subversive. Like a frenemy, it is often implying—through the lens of "concern" or "caring"—that you are not enough.

## We Don't Need the Arrows

You might wonder, *Don't I need that harsh inner voice to push me?* Some of us worry that if we're not hard on ourselves, we might lose our edge or not get results. Research shows the opposite is true: cultivating a compassionate inner voice actually *strengthens* willpower and allows us to take greater risks in pursuit of our goals.

In one illuminating study, the psychologists Claire Adams at Louisiana State University and Mark Leary at Duke University asked young women who were watching their weight to each eat a donut, then drink a full glass of water. The intention was to make the participants feel uncomfortably full, triggering guilt and negative self-talk. The women were then led to another room to sample candy. On the way, half of them received a subtle message of self-compassion. "Everyone indulges sometimes," the facilitator said. "Don't be too hard on yourself." The other half of the women were given no message. Ultimately, the women who received the message of self-compassion ate only twenty-eight grams of candy, compared to their counterparts who ate seventy grams (a difference of approximately *ten* Hershey's Kisses!).[3] The message of self-forgiveness actually **increased** willpower.

In a related research study, participants were offered a tempting piece of chocolate cake. Participants who practiced self-appreciation were four times as likely to resist the cake than those who were shamed. Even those in a control group, given no message, were **twice as likely** to resist compared to the shamed group.[4] This means you would be better off **doing nothing** than criticizing yourself! With self-compassion you have a greater intrinsic motivation and more resilience. Additional research demonstrates that personal standards remain **just as high** when people practice self-compassion, but individuals are not as upset when, for whatever reason, they don't meet those standards.[5]

Self-compassion has been found to reduce anxiety, depression, stress, rumination, perfectionism, body shame, and fear of failure. In case you need more reasons to jump on the bandwagon, self-compassion has also been proven to increase satisfaction, happiness, optimism, curiosity, creativity, and gratitude. I'll have what she's having!

Years ago, I was on a retreat with Kristin Neff, the leading researcher on self-compassion, who stressed the vast chasm between self-compassion and self-esteem. She shared that self-esteem inherently implies a perception of oneself as special, but we can't *always* be above average. It's contingent on outcome and performance (sometimes in comparison to others) and is thus unstable.

If you're an overachiever conditioned to be dependent on external validation, you may have felt your self-worth plummet if you failed or underperformed. Self-esteem's precariousness may have dissuaded you from taking risks (like the woman in Austin who told me she didn't have hobbies for fear of being bad at anything). Many perfectionist overachievers (like me) who were taught to cultivate self-esteem when it was on trend in education go into a shame spiral when we underperform.

Here's the exciting news: self-compassion offers the **same benefits** as high self-esteem but without the downside. Researchers discovered that we subject ourselves to fewer social comparisons and less ego-defensive anger when we practice self-compassion.[6] In contrast to self-esteem, self-compassion gives people more stable self-worth and has no association with narcissism.

Neff approaches self-compassion from three directions: (1) mindfulness versus overidentification, (2) common humanity versus isolation, and (3) self-kindness versus self-judgment.[7]

## 1. Mindfulness versus Overidentification

According to Neff, the first component of developing self-compassion is that when you have a difficult moment or experience, you *notice* you are being hard on yourself. You have the mindfulness skills to name it and say, *Oh, this is a moment of suffering* rather than believing the stories your mind makes up or believing the difficult emotion *is* you. Mindfulness allows you to sit with and observe the painful feelings as they are and witness that inner roommate rather than believe its drama.

The next time you're having a hard time, see if you can simply name it by saying, *There goes my inner roommate again.* You'll immediately pop yourself into mindfulness rather than overidentification.

## 2. Common Humanity versus Isolation

The second component of developing self-compassion is acknowledging your common humanity. Common humanity means seeing your experience as part of a larger human experience and recognizing that other people have suffered like you. You acknowledge that life is hard and imperfect for everyone at different times.

I don't know about you, but sometimes when I'm having a hard time, on some unconscious level my ego wants me to feel *special* in my suffering. For now, simply recognize these victimized thoughts and remind yourself that you're not alone. Other people have suffered in the same way.

### 3. Self-Kindness versus Self-Judgment

The third component of developing self-compassion is relying on self-kindness rather than self-judgment. This involves treating yourself with care and understanding rather than harsh criticism. It also means actively soothing and comforting yourself. You can do this in really simple ways—for example, putting your hands on your chest and saying, "It's okay. You'll get through this."

Remember the other highly effective (and quick!) strategy is to imagine a close friend or loved one is going through the same difficulty. What would you say to them? Write down or imagine the conversation in your mind. Then offer those *same* kind words to yourself.

Using the frumpy and friendless example from earlier, if my best friend told me she felt like a loser driving home from preschool drop-off, here's what I would have told her: "You are NOT a loser! Of course, you want to wear sweatpants. It's exhausting to put on mascara and cute yoga clothes every morning, but if you *did* choose to get all dolled up, you'd look fabulous too. And you've made lots of good friends in your new neighborhood! Besides, it only takes one really good friend to fill your heart. And you're my best friend in the whole world! You are an awesome mom and a kick-ass business owner, and you have so much to be proud of."

I already feel better just having written those words. And when I actually imagine my best friend saying those words to me, it is like applying a salve straight on my soul. It works every time.

## Change Will Trigger Your Inner-Critic Alarm Bells

When you explore The Soul Solution—and anytime you are about to try something new—your inner critic will get *louder*. This is your brain's attempt to keep you safe, even if you're unhappy in your current circumstances. This is just part of the growth process. So, say to yourself, *Oh, there goes that inner voice again, but the house is not really on fire. All is well. I am safe, and I can take risks.*

Your progress may feel slow, but you will get the hang of this. Then you'll lose sight of your new awareness and fall in the hole again before climbing back out. Just remember, this is all part of the process. See if you can be kind, patient, and gentle with yourself. See if you can laugh at the ridiculousness of falling in the same hole again and again. You can feel secure in the knowledge that once you have these Soul Solution tools, you *always* have access to them and can keep coming back as needed. Remember, whether it's the seventeenth or thirty-seventh arrow that you notice, as soon as you stop shooting arrows, you're back on track!

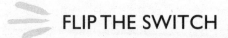

# FLIP THE SWITCH

## Common Self-Critical Patterns

Now that you have an understanding of self-compassion, I'd like to offer you another framework to deal with the common fears of laziness, guilt, and selfishness that crop up in perfectionistic, busy women. Here are some common self-critical patterns you may relate to:

### I'm a Slacker

When women who have been running a million miles an hour start to slow down, their inner critics have a field day, accusing them of being lazy. In order to quit the constant hustle and still live your dreams, you'll need to learn to dismantle this voice.

### Antidote

**Give yourself permission to be a slacker.** Remember when you were a child and your parents would write you a note for school? Well, now your higher self (soul) is giving the tired, overwhelmed, go-go-go (ego) part of you permission to take it easy and get your needs met.

### Instructions

Get out a piece of paper.

Write "I give (your name) permission to _____."

Sign and date the permission slip to make it look official.

Example permission slips:

I give Amy permission to be a slacker.

I give Alka permission to get her needs met.

I give Tanisha permission to rest, and to honor that rest is work.

I give Maneesha permission to not do it all.

I give Alicia permission to read a book/watch TV/go on a walk *before* all her work is done.

Put your permission slip somewhere you'll see it—on your nightstand, next to your computer, or taped to your bathroom mirror—and read it several times a day to remind yourself of this new priority. As the donut and chocolate cake studies suggest, your willpower will be even greater when you cut yourself some slack.

### Antidote Affirmation

Use this affirmation whenever you feel anxious about falling behind:

*I am exactly where I need to be.*

*I am exactly where I need to be.*

*I am exactly where I need to be.*

## Compassion Is Selfish and Overindulgent

Begin to reframe selfishness as being self-full, meaning that you are filling yourself up with what you need so that you can show up as your biggest, brightest self. This is how you can best support others too. As flight attendants say, "Please put your own oxygen mask on first, before assisting others." It's the same with you. You must get your needs met in order to be there for others. If other people call you selfish because you won't do what *they* want, who is really being selfish?

### Antidote Affirmations

*I deserve to have my needs met.*

*I take really good care of myself and that allows me to take really good care of others.*

*I commit to taking really good care of myself and honoring my needs.*

## #FirstWorldProblems and Scales of Suffering

People often confuse self-compassion with self-pity. One major objection I hear from highly resourced women in developed countries is, "I know a lot of other people have it way worse than I do, and I shouldn't complain." This is another excuse to flagellate and deny ourselves the self-compassion we need. There are no scales of suffering; it's not a competition.

You're allowed to have difficult moments even if they feel trivial or privileged. Difficult moments are difficult moments. When you deny your own painful experience and push it down deeper, you don't heal or release it. When you deny your pain, you are also denying your power and your truth. Those small, seemingly insignificant moments of suffering contain important information about what really matters to you. So, pay attention!

### Antidote Self-Compassion Practice

*This is difficult for me. Other people have this difficulty too.*

*This is a moment of suffering. Let me be kind to myself.*

*What is this pain trying to tell me about my deeper needs?*

## From Critic to Coach

When you listen to the self-critical voice in your head, it activates your threat defense system, releasing stress hormones of cortisol and adrenaline into your body. In contrast, when you practice self-compassion and access your inner ally, you activate your physiological mammalian caregiving system and release the feel-good hormone oxytocin and opiates.[8]

## Turn Your Inner Critic into Your Inner Coach

Imagine you're about to take a risk and ask for a raise or attend a party where you know no one.

### Step 1: Get to Know Your Inner Critic

What does your inner critic say in these types of situations? Journal in their voice. What are their "top hits"? What's on their repeat playlist? Paint a picture of the critic. Can you see a face or character that represents them? Give your inner critic a playful name, such as "Perfectionist Polly" or "Judgment Jerry." The better you know them, the more easily you can recognize when your inner critic is driving the bus.

### Step 2: Take Back the Steering Wheel

Start to notice when your inner critic is driving the bus, and physically replace them at the wheel. Physically hold your hands on an imaginary steering wheel in front of you and remove them as you ask your inner critic to step back. Thank them for the input, but firmly tell them they're not currently needed. Shake or wiggle your hands and body to reset, and then imagine handing the wheel to your inner coach instead.

### Step 3: Access Your Wise Inner Coach

Imagine a friend of yours in that same situation. What would you say to them?

Write that down. Then offer those same kind words to yourself.

Listen to the Self-Compassion Guided Meditation at vanessaloder.com/book.

## Soul Symbol

### Ahau
(pronounced a-how')

This symbol represents the cultivation of wholeness and unconditional love. Breathe in and out deeply while gazing at this
symbol and say to yourself, *May all beings feel safe and protected.*
*May all beings be held in loving-kindness. May I forgive, release,*
*and love all beings, including myself.*

I accept and allow myself as I am.

I say yes to embodying unconditional love.

# Chapter 9

# WHAT LIMITS YOU?

A good friend of mine desperately wanted to quit her job, but the same fear-based thoughts kept paralyzing her:

What if she couldn't find a better job?

What if she regretted the choice?

What if she took a risk, and it didn't pay off?

For years, she did nothing.

After reaching a breaking point, she finally made a big change: she left a secure job and solid paycheck to join a riskier, early-stage business for less money. Now she's more intellectually challenged and energized than she's been in years. She didn't realize how stagnant she felt in her old job until she made the switch. Overall, she's very happy with her choice.

Here's the interesting part: almost everything that could go wrong has gone wrong in the new job. Within a month, my friend's boss was fired. Two months later, a key junior person on the team quit. The company is missing its revenue forecast and in the midst of major cost cutting. The CEO isn't that competent. Despite all this, my friend is thriving.

She'd been mulling over worst-case scenarios for *years*, with her fears preventing her from taking action. Yet when her reality proved less than perfect, it wasn't as big a deal as she'd imagined.

Psychologically and emotionally, we often ascribe greater weight to *perceived* or *projected* scenarios than those we in fact *experience*. The anticipation is the hardest part. Why is that the case? Why do we stay stuck when we're miserable? Why don't we take the actions we *know* will benefit us?

Often our fears, beliefs, and traumas are passed down from generation to generation like fine china and silver serving spoons, yet we never ask, *Is this serving me?* To shift these patterns of devotion, it's important to understand epigenetics and family constellation work (more on that in the resources section).

In a study conducted at Emory School of Medicine in 2013, scientists trained mice to fear the smell of cherry blossoms by pairing the floral odor with a mild electric shock on the foot. (Sorry, mice!) The first-generation offspring of these traumatized mice were raised to adulthood having never been exposed to the scent. Yet when these curious little mice caught a whiff of the cherry-blossom fragrance, they quickly became anxious. Even more fascinating, the second generation (grand mice? Is that a thing?) showed the same odor sensitivity and fear of the cherry smell, demonstrating that traumatic memories and fear can be passed down through *two generations*.[1]

Recent research demonstrates that inherited stress impacts humans as well. Rachel Yehuda, a professor of psychiatry and neuroscience at Icahn School of Medicine at Mount Sinai, discovered that children of Holocaust survivors who had post-traumatic stress disorder (PTSD) were born with low cortisol levels similar to their parents, predisposing them to experience PTSD symptoms as well. Yehuda and her team also found epigenetic tags on the children of Holocaust survivors, influencing how they regulate stress later in life. Yehuda's research is groundbreaking in that it demonstrates how descendants of survivors carry the physical and emotional symptoms of traumas they have not experienced firsthand.[2]

Ancestral trauma and experiences within your family lineage offer important context to understanding your life. Perhaps some of your struggles and seemingly default reactions are related to a larger pattern. Begin by getting curious: What were some of the challenges your ancestors faced, and how might that be impacting you today? Were there traumatic events or experiences of exclusion in your family's history? Are there any patterns from childhood that you seem to keep reliving? Use the resources section at the end of this book, particularly Mark Wolynn's book, *It Didn't Start with You*, to go deeper with this crucial work.

*Quick Soul Tip*

A powerful embodiment practice to heal from the past, which I learned from Gay and Katie Hendricks, is to connect with a painful memory from childhood—for example, being bullied at school—and then do this exercise.

Stand up and face a direction in the room that feels like the past to you. Facing the past, extend your arm with your pointer finger outstretched and, as you recall the painful memory, say aloud, "That was then." Continue to repeat this phrase, emphasizing different words, until you feel an energetic or emotional release. "*That* was then. That *was* then. That was *then*." Next, turn in a different direction to face the present, extend your arm, and say aloud, "*This* is now. This *is* now. This is *now*." Repeat until it feels complete.

To finish, face the same direction that represents the past, extend your arm with your pointer finger outstretched, and say out loud, "*That* was them. That *was* them. That was *them*." Once this feels complete, face the present again, and instead of pointing away from yourself, point to your own chest as you repeat, "*This* is me. This *is* me. This is *me*."

Getting curious about your recurring patterns or pain points is the first step toward answering a fundamental question en route to following your True North Star:

What's stopping you from getting
(more of) what you want in life?

## What Is a Limiting Belief?

Do you ever feel stuck in a pattern of behavior that feels bigger than you? Maybe you want to stop pushing yourself so hard at work, learn to create boundaries, or quit snapping at your kids, but despite your best efforts, you can't seem to make a change.

In many cases, old programming and unconscious family loyalty are running the show. A vital step in finding your particular Soul Solution is questioning your limiting beliefs in order to shift your mindset and intentionally choose your path forward.

A limiting belief is any belief that is too small to hold all that you are. As you grow and evolve, you'll continually discover defunct perspectives that you're ready to shed like old skin. These beliefs are remnants from who you *were* (that might have served you at one time), but they are not representative of who you're *becoming*.

Here's a simple and poignant example: No one thought it was possible for a human being to run a four-minute mile. Once someone finally *did* break that record, several other athletes broke the record too, immediately afterward. The old belief was disproved, which shifted people's assumptions about their own capabilities and freed them to succeed.

One easy way to identify when you are under the influence of a limiting belief is the presence of either/or comparisons and black-and-white thinking: *I can have this or that, but not both—my career* or *a good relationship with a loving partner; money* or *creativity; freedom* or *marriage.*

When I left a secure job to follow my energetic bread crumbs and realized I might want to switch careers to leadership coaching, one of my first limiting thoughts was, *Oh great—so now I'm probably going to make less money.* I thought that I could *either* work in finance and make a lot of money *or* find creative work I loved. Rich tycoon or starving artist. It felt like a binary choice with nothing in between.

Anytime you are thinking either/or, pause to ask yourself, *Hmmm, what is the limiting belief underneath this thought pattern?* The Source Your Beliefs Tool at the end of chapter 5 can help you identify some of the unconscious beliefs that may be impacting you.

## One Solution to Limiting Beliefs: Role Models

The quickest way to respond to a limiting belief is to identify it and then intentionally seek out role models who counter it. When it came to the four-minute mile, seeing living proof that the record could be broken propelled several other athletes to achieve the same supposedly impossible goal. When I recognized my own limiting belief about financial versus creative rewards, I decided to seek out role models who had achieved both. I found coaches, healers, and inspirational speakers who were making a great living, writing books, giving keynote speeches, and running large corporate trainings and massive online courses. Suddenly I had a much bigger vision for the business I was creating.

I took some of these programs so that I could learn from these potential role models firsthand. Some didn't seem to embody what they taught (which taught me valuable lessons about discernment and constantly updating my role-model criteria); others amazed me and became incredible mentors. But my journey to amend limiting beliefs didn't stop there: Years later, I was struggling with the perceived trade-offs of growing my business, spending more time with my kids, and finding alone time to recharge my battery. I felt like something had to give, until I talked to a very successful teacher of mine, who has a growing business, spends plenty of time with her young daughter, and takes **one whole day a week just for herself!** What?! That knowledge stretched my perceptions and broke my limits, for sure!

As I learned how she was balancing the various aspects of her life, it encouraged me to be more protective with my leisure time. In the past, I'd taken days off to spend with my kids, but it had seemed overly indulgent to take *another day* just for myself. At first I only took ten or fifteen minutes for myself, once or twice a week (not including self-care or working out; this was pure, unstructured alone time). Gradually I built up to one to two hours. One day I hope to get to a place where I take a full day just for myself every week. Meanwhile, my role model inspires me to keep moving toward that goal.

No matter what your goal, seek out role models who have achieved what you are hoping to do. In parenting, a lot of us have been taught to act like martyrs, constantly sacrificing our needs. To counteract this cultural pressure, I seek out role models who seem to have a more relaxed parenting style that includes plenty of self-care.

Another pro tip is to set specific intentions with any mentors you meet with regularly. "I reached out to a senior leader in my company to help navigate relationship issues at work (i.e., how to have difficult conversations with managers and peers)," my client Alicia described. "We would meet once a month over lunch. Before starting, we each established what we wanted to get out of the meetings. It was a very valuable experience." You might be surprised how much information people are willing to share if you're specific about your interests (versus saying you'd like to learn from them in general, which can be overwhelming in its vagueness).

Lastly, your role models don't have to be people you personally know. You can choose historical or well-known contemporary figures who inspire you. On my altar above where I meditate, I have a candle featuring a picture of RBG (Ruth Bader Ginsburg) that brings a huge smile to my heart. When I want to call on fierce, feminine, world-changing energy, I light that candle and imagine RBG joining me in whatever I'm doing. It feels amazing. I have also called on the energy, inspiration, and examples of Joan of Arc, Gloria Steinem, Maya Angelou, Oprah Winfrey, Quan Yin, the Egyptian goddess Isis (she's helping me write this book!), the archangel Michael, St. Germain, the Council of Light and the Blue Council (groups of light beings), and many others. Whoever you choose as your role models, the point is to channel their wisdom and gifts to guide you forward.

## Calling on Role Models

The next time you want to feel supported—perhaps in a difficult conversation or taking a risk at work—take a few minutes to ground yourself and repeat these phrases: "I, (*your name*), align with the light of love, wisdom, and truth. I call on my higher self to join me. I call on the energy of (role model) to join me in this endeavor. Help me to (*your goal*)."

For example,

> *I, Vanessa Loder, align with the light of love, wisdom, and truth. I call on my higher self and solar angel to join me. I call on the wisdom and grace of Isis. Help me to be a clear channel for insights, joy, ease, and clarity of thought throughout this writing process. And so it is. Aho.*

## Small "Soul Steps"

Another strategy that will help you overcome limiting beliefs and move beyond your trepidation is to take consistent, small, imperfect actions. Ask yourself, *What is one thing I can do today to move this idea or project forward?*

For three years, my client Mollie has wanted to quit her job as a VP of marketing to pursue a career in fine art, but she's been terrified about making the transition. Now she's finally ready to take the leap. When I asked what most helped her get there, she explained that taking lots of small actions added up to massive change over time. Mollie began by taking free audio classes on Skillshare—which she listened to on long walks—to learn new artistic skills, such as how to produce colorful patterns and how to monetize creativity. That same platform also enabled her to find role models who were making a living in this new field. She began to feel inspired by their experiences and see a path forward. Mollie also committed to painting five nights a week after her kids went to bed. Over several months, she built a portfolio. Mollie's consistent daily actions allowed her to gain momentum, confidence, and a sense of progress and preparation as she moved toward this daunting goal.

## Feel the Fear, but Don't Believe Fear's Story

When I first graduated from business school, I thought about doing something entrepreneurial, but I chickened out. I had a very rational-sounding reason: I figured I should go back to private equity to pay off my student loans. In hindsight, it was actually fear of failure that stopped me.

Fear can stop us from living our best and truest lives. Why is our terror stronger than our ability to choose what we *know* will make us happier? Why are we operating based on an outdated survival instinct that doesn't consider our overall well-being?

As I mentioned, when I confronted my fears about marriage with help from an executive coach, the fear itself did not disappear completely. I just learned how to breathe through it and observe rather than believe the scary narratives that my mind would shout at me: *Most marriages end in divorce! What if he's not the one or you grow apart ten years from now?*

Fear often sounds very logical, but it ends up making you feel hopeless and trapped. One helpful tactic is to begin to recognize and label the voice of fear.

What if you could treat fear as a source of humor or endearment rather than being rattled by it? Those of you who watched *Saturday Night Live* in the early aughts may recall a character named Debbie Downer whose constant negativity about things such as the risk of feline AIDS (number one killer of domestic cats) becomes so ridiculous that you can't help but laugh. Imagine treating your own fear in a similar fashion, noticing how extreme or constant its utterings are and thinking to yourself, *Oh, silly fear! There you go again!*

Start by asking, *Hmmm, what is the positive intention this fear has for me?* Maybe it wants to protect you from feeling rejected or hurt. Maybe fear has prevented you from taking risks outside your comfort zone in an attempt to keep you safe. Identifying the positive intention behind your fear can help you begin to have empathy for the fear (and for yourself).

When you have an emotion or experience you don't like, if you try to conquer it, push it down, or stifle it, you'll stay stuck in a loop. As the Swiss psychologist Carl Jung famously shared, "what you resist, persists." And as Katie Hendricks often says, "all our feelings come out of the same faucet. If you clamp down on fear or anger, you also clamp down on joy and love." The best way to work with fear is to allow yourself to feel it. Breathe into the fear and give yourself a couple minutes for the physiological symptoms to pass while you refuse to believe the stories it's telling you. Then befriend your fear. Get to know it. Treat it like a wounded child and see what it needs from you.

## Befriend Your Feelings

Try this wonderful practice from Gay and Katie Hendricks: Imagine a park bench or a porch swing, located somewhere beautiful and peaceful in nature. Next, see or sense yourself sitting on this bench or swing with your fear (or sadness or anger) next to you. If this feeling had a color, what color would it be? Notice what shape or texture it takes. Is it a brown blob or an orange spiky ball? Allow whatever your imagination creates.

Now, befriend this feeling. Take your arm and gently put it around the fear, or reach out your hand with your palm up and invite the fear to hold your hand. Just sit quietly on the bench together for a peaceful moment with your arm around it or holding hands.

When you're ready, look into fear's eyes and ask, *What do you need from me?* It might want a hug or for you to keep holding its hand. Perhaps it just wants you to say "I love you" or "I appreciate you." Give fear whatever it needs and then notice what happens. Even if this is uncomfortable, see if you can honor the feeling and offer it whatever it needs. The fear may change shapes or colors. It may want to throw a temper tantrum and destroy something, so you and fear go throw rocks off a cliff together. Back on the bench, maybe fear wants to rest its head in your lap. Allow your imagination to flow from image to image, simply observing what happens. Keep working with the emotions until you feel complete. You may go through several iterations.[3]

This exercise works for other emotions as well. "When I did Befriend Your Feelings, frustration showed up and just needed to have a little fun," said my client Emily. "So I put him in front of *Will & Grace* reruns while I worked. It helps so much."

This tool is a powerful way to personify some of your difficult emotions and work with them in a loving and supportive manner rather than negating or (unsuccessfully) ignoring them. Try the practice for yourself and see what you notice. While it's lovely to read about these exercises, you must actually *do them* to receive the benefit.

## Fear, Jealousy, and a Wild Little Girl

None of us are immune to comparing ourselves to others, thereby compounding a fear of inadequacy. I've personally gone into downward spirals comparing myself to other teachers—for example: How many people have taken my class? How many five-star reviews have I received? These insecurities only exacerbated my shame, especially as my mission is to help other women, and I was secretly jealous of other female teachers' success. Even knowing how terrible this made me feel, I often couldn't resist the temptation to check what other people were doing. Female competition is a very old current of energy that runs in many of us—but it can be shifted.

As I dug into my patterning to uncover what this dynamic was really about, I realized it was rooted in how my mom would continually pit me and my sister against each other. She would alternately favor one of us as "the good one" for a period of time before haphazardly shifting her affections. It was really confusing to navigate. My grandmother was even more manipulative, so my mom came by this pattern naturally. But that didn't make it any less painful.

One particular morning, despite awareness about the root of these feelings, I caught myself in a full-on jealous spiral and despaired. After two years of observing this pattern, I wanted to be done with it!

Getting still and quiet, I asked myself, *Why do I keep this drama going and continue to beat myself up in this way?* Underneath all the hurt and betrayal was a core limiting belief that I wasn't good enough. While our experiences are all different, many of us share this sense of inadequacy. Working with our inner child is a powerful way to shift this old belief.

Closing my eyes, I took myself through a visualization to visit that wounded little girl. In a dimly lit cave was a filthy child dressed in rags, her hair wild and unkempt, and she was crouching on the ground. I began to coax her into the light, imagining perhaps I could bathe her and offer her clean clothes. She became furious at this suggestion, saying that I was trying to manipulate her. "Get the f*ck out of my cave!" she yelled. She was wild and wanted to stay that way.

This part of me was in such deep pain. She did not feel seen, valued, or accepted as she was. So, I spent time with her in the cave, drawing in the dirt, not asking her to change. I got filthy with her. Eventually she came out into the light with me, squinting from the brightness. I was careful not to ask her to clean up or change in any way. She chose to remain dirty in her rags, and we spent time together in nature. Slowly she began to trust me. Through self-guided visualizations, I visited with her every night for a week and then off and on again whenever I felt the need.

One afternoon after leading an inner child visualization with a group of clients, I was on a neighborhood walk and passed a field with hundreds of tiny yellow wildflowers in bloom. Suddenly the wild girl from the cave whispered directly in my ear: "I would like one of those." So I picked a tall stem for her and carried it with me the rest of the walk.

As I gazed at the flower in a ceramic vase that week, I felt a profound sense of love and self-acceptance. Now whenever I see wildflowers on my walk, I ask that girl if she wants me to bring her one. Sometimes when I'm at the grocery store, I ask if she'd like me to get her anything. Occasionally she has a clear request for dark chocolate. You, too, can spend time with your wild little girl and give her the mothering you needed. This is a deeply healing experience.

We each have a little child inside of us with particular wounds and needs specific to our childhood experiences. Sometimes you may think you understand an issue only to discover your inner child or wounded part has new information that unlocks what you need to release the past and move forward. Now, anytime I get triggered comparing myself to others—I can't resist the temptation to check social media to see what someone else is doing—I check in with that wild girl. Usually she is in pain. I spend time loving her and accepting her the way she is until it feels complete. My personal triggers offer a hidden gift of healing by shining a light on the places within me that feel inadequate and need to feel loved. I will know this part has been healed and transmuted when what used to trigger me one day no longer does. Until then, I'll keep bringing her flowers.

## You Are Not Responsible for Your Parents' Dreams

My client Leia is a driven woman whose bubbly Energizer Bunny personality uplifts others. When she was younger, Leia loved learning about exercise and nutrition, but she sublimated her passion in order to please her immigrant parents and chose finance instead. Depleted and unfulfilled, Leia was eager to confront the old beliefs and family loyalties that had guided her decisions.

Leia examined her current beliefs about money, career, and being a working woman by completing these sentences that you'll recognize from chapter 5:

*What my mom says about money/career/working women . . .*

*What my dad says about money/career/working women . . .*

*What society says about money/career/working women . . .*

She was surprised when an old high school memory surfaced in which she confided in her mother that she loved fitness, only to be admonished for impractical career choices. Recalling this memory allowed Leia to begin to heal from her past and identify an energetic bread crumb she was excited to pursue.

After recognizing the hidden beliefs that were running her life, Leia consciously chose to cultivate new values. She spent time visualizing and writing her own script. Once she had completed this process, she finally felt free to pursue certification as a fitness instructor and began training other burned-out coworkers during their lunch break. The transition felt effortless. One day, Leia was changing into her workout clothes in the locker room of her office building's gym when some women approached her to ask how she got so fit. These were Leia's first official clients. While it was challenging for Leia to confront and dismantle her parents' beliefs about what a "meaningful" career looks like, it was well worth it. Now she's training to be a bodybuilder and launching a fitness coaching business on the side. Like Leia, with time and work, we can release our limiting beliefs and create our own set of values and goals, free from influence.

# FLIP THE SWITCH

Supplemental supportive materials are available on my website vanessaloder.com/book, including a Befriend Your Feelings Guided Meditation, to work with fear in a productive way.

## Inner Child Meditation

As we start, tune in to something painful or difficult in your life—something that has been showing up in your experience lately or that is a recurring complaint, a situation that your mind has been stuck on and you can't seem to shift. This could be a struggle in a certain relationship or something with your work or health. Simply choose a current struggle and begin to tune in to it. It probably feels bad. Imagine yourself in that situation now. What are some of the thoughts that you're thinking about yourself or this other person or the world that are so painful for you?

Allow yourself to just feel the sensations in your body. What does it feel like? Where do you feel it the most? Is there a tightness in your chest, a constriction in your throat, or a numbness in your belly? Where is the epicenter of these feelings in your body? In your heart, solar plexus, or stomach? Simply notice and observe the physical sensations.

Now, remember that underneath your current struggle is a very old pain. There's a much younger part of you that's feeling upset or sad. Connect with that part by asking yourself this question from Katie and Gay Hendricks: *Hmmm, when have I felt this way before? How is this feeling familiar, this tightness in my chest (or whatever sensations you are observing)?* You might imagine yourself as a little girl, hunched over in a protective posture, or you might see a part that's not human, like a caricature or cartoon, or you may just have a feeling.

Connect with the part of you that's inside of all that pain. If it is a little girl, how old is she? If you aren't sure, tune in to the physical sensations in your body and ask yourself, *When is the first time I felt this pain, this tightness in my chest? This feeling of not being good enough, or feeling unsafe?* Whatever the pain is, how old were you when you first felt it?

Gently invite that little girl or that part forward. She might be crouching in a dark corner, hiding, feeling ashamed or upset, angry or scared. Just take a moment and see if you can coax her out. Invite her to join you. There may be a protective part who is guarding her that you need to communicate with and heal first. If needed, you can talk to that part and ask it what it is protecting you from. Once the little girl is willing to speak with you, ask her, "What do you need?"

She might ask you to leave her alone. If that's the case, you can just let her know that you're here and you'll wait quietly and patiently for her until she's ready. Say, "I'm here for you now, and I can give you what you need."

Next, do one of the two following practices: either the somatic practice, which I learned from Mark Wolynn, or the intuitive practice, listening to your own inner guidance.

## Somatic Practice

Tune in to the painful experience and reconnect with the places in your body where you feel any sensations or numbness. Place your hands on the areas in your body where you feel tightness, constriction, numbness, or any other sensations. For example, you may place one hand on your chest where you feel tightness and the other hand on your belly where you feel numbness.

If you don't feel anything, just place your hand where you imagine or sense the feelings to be. Breathe into those areas. To activate your parasympathetic nervous system, allow your mouth to be open about one-quarter inch and place your tongue on the roof of your mouth at the back of your teeth. Relax and drop your hamstring and quadricep muscles to open the pelvic floor. Then say, "I've got you." Imagine there is a child part of you that has been waiting for you to notice them, and today is the day. Continue by saying the following phrases: "I've got you. I'll breathe with you, all of you, until you feel held and seen and safe. I'll breathe with you until you're calm, until we integrate back in our core as particles of energy moving in an infinity symbol." Then breathe with the sensations until you feel a shift. Hold the infinity sign as a sensation; no mind, no thought. Do this practice six times a day for at least sixty seconds to change the brain.

## Intuitive Practice

Continue to ask your inner little girl what she needs and then give her whatever she wants. Maybe she would like a hug or for you to get her a cup of warm milk. So you do. Or perhaps she's angry and wants to go destroy something, so you offer her a sledgehammer, and the two of you go smash some windows together. Maybe she wants to build a fort with pillows and blankets and then wants you both to get inside to feel really cozy, safe, and warm.

Spend a few minutes doing whatever she wants and giving her whatever she needs to feel safe and secure. There may be some words or phrases that come to you to say to her. You can go ahead and say those as well.

Do whatever she needs to feel safe, loved, seen, and heard.

Next, visualize or imagine that there's a beautiful magical place nearby. It could be a magical house, a castle that's up on a hill, or a special fort inside a tree house. Whatever it is, find this beautiful magical place that's just for her.

Walk with her to the entrance of this magical place. Inside are guides, light beings, or angels. When she gets to the door and steps inside this beautiful magical place, she's welcomed and greeted with love and caring by these beings of light. Inside are all her favorite toys, all her favorite games and things to do, and there are lots of beings there who love her and care about her. These could be relatives who have passed on or light beings or just imaginary beings. They're all excited to see her, saying, "Welcome! Welcome! We're so glad you're here." They give her a tour and show her around. They have set up a cozy spot and a plate with all her favorite snacks. They say, "We're going to take really good care of you here."

Once she's settled, you let her know, "You'll be safe here and I'll come back and visit you whenever you want." If she gets nervous about you leaving, create a little room inside your heart space for her. Tell her, "You can come stay in my heart if you want or you can stay here in this magical place. There will always be a room for you inside my heart. I can talk to you whenever you want."

If she wants, she can shrink down really small and have this little space inside your heart where you hold her. Or she can stay in this magical place. She can go back and forth as she pleases. She's free to do whatever she wants.

Now it's time to bring your visit with her to a close. Let her know that you'll come and check on her anytime she wants, and she can always stay inside your heart. She might ask for you to check on her tomorrow or at least once a week. Say your goodbyes with love, leaving her with the guides and light beings in her magical place or in your heart. Come back to this present moment in your physical body, wiggling your fingers and toes. As you're ready, allow your eyes to gently open.

You now have processes to work with difficult emotions, heal your inner child, and identify some of the core fears and limiting beliefs that have kept you stuck in the past—woo hoo! Remember to do a little happy dance every time you notice a pattern that's no longer serving you because it means you're on the path to changing it.

## Soul Symbol

## Hologram

This symbol represents releasing yourself from self-limitations and old stories that you are imperfect and unworthy. As you access a broader perspective of the larger hologram, you can sense that your "mistakes" or "issues" are part of a larger story. Breathe in and out as you remind yourself, *My external reality is a mirror showing me the changes needed to bring me into alignment.*

All my experiences are gifts for my evolution into wholeness.

I say yes to the bigger story of my life.

# Chapter 10

# THE SUCCESS MYTH

**M**ost of us know Arianna Huffington as a cofounder of the Huffington Post and founder/CEO of Thrive Global, as well as one of *Time* magazine's "most influential people." According to our traditional definition of success, Arianna has crushed it.

But she also worked so tirelessly that she woke up in a pool of her own blood. She'd been pushing herself so hard that she finally collapsed, hitting her head on the corner of her office desk. When she awoke on the floor with a gaping head wound, she was struck by a single thought: "*This is success?*"[1]

Arianna had followed the old rules based on the traditional paradigm of success, cranking as hard as possible to climb the proverbial (ahem, *patriarchal*) ladder. But this incident changed her perspective. She quickly became an advocate for redefining success and even wrote *Thrive*, a book encouraging people to cultivate more holistic and balanced lives.

Not everyone has a turning point that dramatic. Instead, most of us have a subtle but persistent sense that something is off. We find ourselves thinking things like:

*I just know in my bones I am meant for something more.*

*I feel a vague sense of dissatisfaction that I can't really pinpoint.*

*This "success" isn't sustainable.*

Though those revelations—or soul whispers—may not be as resounding as literally being hit over the head with the truth, quiet inklings about our notions of success matter. Part of The Soul Solution process is learning to recognize and honor your own subtle cues and sophisticated abilities of discernment. It's also about recognizing that not all the obstacles are internal: Maybe things feel "off" because the system itself is off, not because something is wrong with you. Maybe you're beginning to sense that this playbook was not written for you or in your favor.

## What Is the Success Myth?

For ages, our culture has embraced an outdated definition of success, including an obsession with productivity and wearing "busy" as a badge of honor. As women, we also suffer from "human giver syndrome," feeling pressure to achieve the Gold Standards in all areas at once, and the inherent self-doubt that comes from living in a patriarchal culture that devalues many feminine traits and encourages rational, logical thinking over body wisdom and intuition. Many of us feel the ramifications of that every day, and yet concretizing a new definition of success feels insurmountable.

Maneesha, a senior leader at Morgan Stanley, recently said to me,

> *My career has been very successful on the surface, but [recently], when the firm talked about promoting me, it just didn't feel right in my body. When I explain this to people, they think I'm opting for the "mommy track," and assume changing my paradigm of success means stepping back. But it doesn't have to [mean that]. I want to build a company that is meaningful to me. I want to show my girls it's possible to own your own success.*

Despite Maneesha's strong principles and perspective, she accepted the promotion at first. Change is difficult. The myth tells us there's only one way to be successful, and it involves burning the candle at both ends until we don't even know what our goals are anymore. The truth is, women are often canaries in the coal mine, demonstrating that our corporate and social structures are failing us. After all, the current system was set up by (white) men for (white) men. The disconnect between your authentic self and the dictates of society feels that much more pronounced when you are born in a female body (or any marginalized body or identity) within a patriarchal structure.

As we begin to come together and express these truths, our world will change. In her book *The Creation of Patriarchy*, Gerda Lerner wisely writes,

> *Men and women live on a stage. . . . But the stage set is conceived, painted, defined by men. . . . It takes considerable time for the women to understand that getting "equal" parts will not make them equal, as long as the script, the props, the stage setting, and the direction are firmly held by men. When the women begin to realize that and cluster together between the acts . . . this play comes to an end.*[2]

Women have been conditioned for millennia to distrust our own impulses and accept ingrained cultural norms around achievement. Part of finding The Soul Solution involves bringing these nagging feelings about success to the surface and honoring the profound wisdom they convey.

For many of us, waking up to the reality of our own work-life imbalance is a foggy experience full of second-guessing. For me, it was an anticlimactic moment (or series of moments) that seismically shifted my perspective.

Shortly after getting back from my honeymoon in 2012, I called the executive coach who had helped me overcome my fear of marriage and expressed similar internal conflict about my work. It was intellectually stimulating. I was on a partner track, making money, and working with people I liked. But, in truth, I actually didn't *want* to be a partner at a private equity firm. I just thought I was supposed to want that.

I thought I was the problem. But, as she helped me see, I was chasing someone else's dreams. I was not alone. The Western world is not set up to support most women's needs—or really the needs of anyone who wants to feel balanced, authentic, and fulfilled. We've been dutifully trying to prove our worthiness and earn other people's approval, acceptance, and love while abandoning ourselves in the process. The solution isn't to strive harder. The Soul Solution that blasts the Success Myth to smithereens is to rip up the old playbook created by men of the past and design a new one, from the inside out. "Perhaps the greatest challenge to thinking women is the challenge to move from the desire for safety and approval to the most 'unfeminine' quality of all—that of intellectual arrogance, the supreme hubris which asserts to itself **the right to reorder the world**," said Lerner. "The hubris of the god makers, the hubris of the male-system builders."[3]

## How Did We Get Into This Mess?

To create a new paradigm of success and leadership, we must first identify the toxic beliefs that have been dominating our cultural landscape.

### Productivity and the Loss of Leisure

One reason women are struggling is because of our culture's obsession with productivity, role overload, and our denigration of leisure as a worthy pursuit. Much of today's Success Myth can be traced back to the Industrial Revolution, accelerated by the current technological revolution.

Did you know that medieval peasants worked, on average, far fewer hours than we do today and that Athenians in ancient Greece enjoyed up to *sixty holidays* a year? In 1930, the economist John Maynard Keynes predicted that by 2030, people would need to work **only fifteen hours a week** in order to be fed, clothed, and housed, and they would have ample time to focus on leisure.[4]

He wasn't the only one who was off base. In her book *Do Nothing*, Celeste Headlee says, "In 1965, a Senate subcommittee predicted that by the year 2000, Americans would work fourteen-hour weeks and take nearly two months of vacation time. Instead, the average American gets ten days of paid vacation and nearly one in four gets no paid holidays at all."[5]

Headlee attributes this disconnect to a rise in consumerism and income inequality.

Basically, workers had a choice to use their extra income to **work less** *or* **buy more**. They were encouraged by our capitalist structures to choose the latter. Why? Because the economy requires growth to keep expanding. So, we became single-mindedly focused on growth without considering other factors such as the degradation of the environment or the well-being of workers. We pursued growth for growth's sake without creating a more holistic definition of the type of growth we wanted to pursue.

### Own Your Needs

Historically, women have found it challenging to claim their authentic needs because of deep (often unconscious) conditioning that we exist to serve others. We have become what Cornell University philosophy professor Kate

Manne calls "human givers" rather than human beings, a class of people who are "expected to offer their time, attention, affection, and bodies willingly, placidly, to the other class of people, the 'human beings.'"[6]

Unwittingly, women in the Western world continue to surrender our power, playing into subservient or inequitable roles. We take on more than our fair share of household and childcare duties, stewing in resentment while ineffectually advocating for equitable partnership. We want meaningful work and are tired of sacrificing our well-being for approval, but we push ourselves to prove we can make it in the boys' club. And since caregiving is devalued in our culture, when we do choose time with our children, we feel compelled to devalue our own choices, joking about "leaning out" to mask our shame for opting out of a system that doesn't support us.

So, we push to prove we can do it all. But pushing is not a recipe for happiness or true success—change is. It's not our fault. Shifting an age-old system is an arduous task, one that we can only achieve together. As we begin to own our true needs and desires, we're able to harness our full capabilities at work and at home. It starts with asking ourselves, *How have I abandoned myself, played into restrictive roles, or subjugated my own needs?*

## Unwinding Success Myth Beliefs

Earlier we discussed how when you label a thought or an emotion, suddenly you no longer *are* that feeling. This brings your awareness back to your core self or soul, which operates at a higher level of consciousness. With the Success Myth, it can be helpful to notice and name some of these old beliefs in order to shift them, putting you back in the seat of the observer. If you know in your gut that something would be beneficial to you and yet you aren't making it a priority, it's often because of old programming. So let's get curious: What are the *beliefs* about success that have kept you from finding The Soul Solution?

Below are some of the current beliefs many people hold about success, work, women, and leadership. Circle the ones that feel the most alive for you today. In some cases, the very act of naming the belief and sourcing its origin will be enough to create radical change. Remember to be kind and playful as you dig into your patterning. Remember what author and success coach Jen Sincero says, "We're all just little bunnies doing our best."[7]

Success requires sacrifice.

Work is serious, not fun and joyful.

The busier I am, the more important I am.

Sleep when you die; rest is for the weak.

Creativity and financial freedom are mutually exclusive.

Prioritizing leisure means you're lazy and unimportant.

Time equals money.

More (output, hours, stuff) is better.

Asking for help is weak.

Competition over collaboration.

Women can only be successful by being like men.

Caregiving is women's work and is less valuable.

What other beliefs do you hold that may no longer be serving you?

After circling the most relevant beliefs, ask yourself:

- *How do I feel when I hold this belief?*
- *What is the cost of operating in this way?*
- *Is this something I want to intentionally choose to believe in moving forward, or would I rather create a new belief structure?*
- *What might be possible if I were free from this belief?*

Many of these beliefs operate in a clandestine way in our subconscious. For example, you might consciously think, *Of course I believe in the importance of rest and renewal!* But when you try to take a break from work, you feel guilty and end up running errands in your spare time. You want to be free from the Success Myth but are also afraid to let it go.

Often we adopt a belief without pausing to consider if we want to intentionally subscribe to it. It's like we accidentally joined a club by being born into a certain family or culture. In some fortunate cases, external circumstances catalyze a cultural shift that forces us to see our old patterns differently. For example, one of the silver linings of COVID-19 is how it shattered the old belief that workers need to be at the office, all day, five days a week, in order to be productive. Suddenly the country collectively saw things differently, which created opportunity for new structures to emerge. Imagine if we could revisit all our beliefs, without the propellant of a global pandemic—we can!!

As we bring these types of conversations to the surface, we begin building the collective change we long to see. We need a community of like-minded allies in this process. It's scary and lonely to take a stand for a new paradigm in a world that may criticize and shame us for stepping out of line.

## The Old versus New Paradigm of Success

Today, more and more conscious leaders are waking up to the fact that our current obsession with growth at any cost is counterproductive. In the new paradigm of success, we create win-win scenarios instead.

Now that you've started to investigate your ingrained beliefs, here are five mindset shifts you can make *immediately* to deprogram the Success Myth:

### Mindset Shift #1—Busy as a Badge of Honor

Have you ever noticed that when you ask "How are you doing?" people often reply, "Busy. Crazy busy." Busy is not actually a feeling. Yet when we have a lot on our calendars, we tend to feel more important. This is more than a little backward. Bringing awareness to this flawed equivalency between busyness and worthiness is a start. Many of us feel powerless to change our situations. At work, the busyness trap has us constantly striving to keep an unsustainable pace. At home, it leaves our children dizzy from the frantic clip and leaves us depleted, resentful, and disconnected from loved ones. Because our society does not implicitly value caregiving, but it *does* value being busy, we cram our days full of activities to show that we, too, deserve credit for a job well done. But this busyness doesn't actually help us feel better.

Here's the real issue: We are all caving into this broader narrative without realizing **we create the narrative.**

This hamster wheel of hustle is ultimately unfulfilling. If your sense of worth is contingent on outside validation and being "busy," **you can never stop.** You never win.

If being busy is the end goal, **there is no end**.

Think about that for a moment.

If your value is based on your level of busyness, you *always* have to be busy to maintain your value. If, on the other hand, your sense of value comes from deep inside, from being present and sharing your gifts and essence with the world, you get to enjoy your life.

But how do we get there? What's the secret to creating more sustainable, soul-centric success?

What if the opposite of busyness isn't laziness but deep stillness and inner quiet? Slowing down and cultivating quiet will help you begin to unwind the busy trap. These are necessary traits if we're to live a life true to our core self.

### Busyness as a Decoy

What if busyness is an **excuse** to mask painful truths and circumvent the scary work of creating change in your life? What if busyness is a form of denial, a sneaky avoidance pretending to do important things on the surface while neglecting the most important work of all—the evolution of your soul?

"What is keeping me from doing LESS?" one client of mine recently asked. "Why won't I say no to some things? *There's a part of me that wants to keep busy because of a fear of being lonely.*" The busier we are, the harder it becomes to pause, check in with ourselves, and ask, *How am I really doing at this moment?*

As you break up with busyness, you may feel panic well up. You may have to face some difficult truths. You might feel sad, depressed, restless, or scared. That's normal.

Simply breathe through it, notice the sensations in your physical body, and allow yourself five to ten minutes of quiet time to do nothing each day. I'm offering you a compassionate hug and an energetic high-five every time you do this.

### Breaking Up with Busyness

Try saying this: "Look, busyness, we've had a good run. Thank you for getting me all those gold stars. I won't lie, I've enjoyed the high from the adrenaline and cortisol I get when we're together. But it's taking a toll. I thought if I were with you, I would matter. But I'm running on fumes. It's time to move on. I'm going to start dating both rest and renewal. If that goes well, I might take things to the next level and start to see nourishment, leisure, and pleasure too."

### Quick Soul Tip

Read these two sentences and notice how you *feel* in your body after each one:

I am busy.

(Check in with your body, how do you *feel*? Is your body tightening up? Is your mind spinning or still?)

I am relaxed.

(Check in with your body, how do you *feel*? Do you feel your body soften? Does your mind begin to quiet?)

The words we tell ourselves about ourselves matter. The words we use to describe ourselves privately and publicly matter. Mind your language and your reality will follow. One very simple yet effective action you can take is to stop saying, "I am busy." Whatever you put after the words "I am" is an affirmation that will become a self-fulfilling prophecy over time. Saying "I am busy" will keep you running in circles instead of finding your path.

Instead, say to yourself:

*I have plenty of time for everything I want and need to do today.*

*There is always time for what is most important to me.*

*I am enough, just as I am.*

*I am exactly where I need to be.*

Try these out for yourself and notice how you feel.

In a culture that rewards output over essence, *doing* more than *being*, and busyness over stillness, breaking up with busyness is a radical act.

### The Cult of Busy Will Try to Hook You Back In

Word of warning: even when you break up with busy, other people will assume you're still a couple. I've tried to remove *busy* from my vocabulary and have noticed how much other people invoke the concept, saying, "You must be crazy busy!" On the days or weeks when I have a lot going on—a book deadline, speaking engagements, kids' activities—I'll simply say, "I'm really *full* this week." It's honest and it feels better to my nervous system, meaning my body feels calmer.

### Mindset Shift #2—From Hustle to Flow

Another powerful mindset shift you can make is to notice when you are in "hustle" mode and intentionally switch to a state of "flow."

A few years ago, I was in the middle of a big launch for an online course and decided, "I'm going to drive to Philz Coffee shop and crank out emails." I parked and was charging down the sidewalk when I caught myself in this combative inner mindset and thought, *Wait. This is not how I want to work anymore.* I stopped in my tracks so suddenly that the woman behind me almost ran smack into me! I marched right back to my car and drove to a nearby yoga class, where I ended up having an inspired idea for the project that increased revenue by 20 percent. (The idea came to me while standing in Warrior 2 pose. Who knew that pose was so lucrative?!)

This moment illustrates a shift from hustle to flow. When we let go of the old impulse to push, we open ourselves up to ease and intuition. We tap into our highest potential, expanding in creativity and abundance, and we feel better more of the time. Similar to the story of the veteran who altered his experience by pausing to label an emotion in the grocery store, I was able to *notice* my hustle, *name* it, and then *choose* a different route to success.

*Quick Soul Tip*

Close your eyes and remember a time when you were in "hustle" mode—rushing around. How did it feel? What do you notice? What was your self-talk? What beliefs come up about yourself or the world?

Then wiggle around to break that state and get back to neutral.

Next, close your eyes and recall a time when you were in flow, fully engaged in whatever you were doing. How did it feel? What do you notice? What were you saying to yourself? What beliefs come up?

One of my clients described being in flow as "calm but focused, playful, relaxed, authentic, energized. Things feel effortless."

Flow feels incredibly good, *and* it allows us to get more done with less effort. Given this, why don't we spend more time in flow every day?

The short answer is we put a limit on how good we allow ourselves to feel due to our unconscious programming around suffering, family loyalty, old pain, and limiting beliefs about worthiness and love. On top of this, research shows a gendered difference in our experience. According to the renowned psychologist Mihaly Csikszentmihalyi, women tend to feel guiltier taking time for themselves to be in flow.[8] Women have been *conditioned* to feel this guilt by broader cultural forces. Little girls don't complain of feeling *guilty* when they play freely any more than little boys do. The exciting implication is that if we have been *taught* this way of being, we can *unlearn* it.

Feel the guilt and do it anyway.

If you feel guilty taking time for yourself, know that you're not alone. If you're struggling with guilt, imagine what a dear friend would say to you and then offer those same words to yourself.

*Flow Is an Empowerment Issue*

Being in flow is an empowerment issue for women. Choose to be in flow as a radical act on behalf of women everywhere. Remember that allowing yourself more time in a flow state is one of the best ways to reclaim your power, creativity, joy, ease, and *success* on your terms.

Human beings were not built to constantly hustle without any breaks in order to be productive. In fact, it's often when your brain is in a relaxed state that you are able to access the best ideas and solutions.

## Mindset Shift #3—From "Always On" to Cycles

When human beings lived in an agrarian society, we worked by the cycles of the sun, the seasons, and the harvest. Focused periods of effort were followed by rest. In today's global economy, many workers sit hunched over screens for ten to twelve hours a day, 365 days a year, rarely getting up to move their bodies. Heck, I rarely take a pee break! There's no supervisor yelling at me to make more widgets, but I have unconsciously internalized this ethos.

Most people understand that staring at a computer screen is not a recipe for enhanced creativity and well-being, but we struggle to pull ourselves away from an "always on," manufacturing-era attitude.

*"Cranking" All the Time = Diminishing Marginal Returns*

In reality, you're not as productive as you think. Research confirms that very few people can concentrate on impactful tasks for more than four or five hours a day in total, including high-achieving authors, musicians, and athletes. Sitting in front of a computer all day is *not* how you optimize your potential and live a satisfied life. Plus, there's a loss of cognitive function if you suffer from sleep deprivation and chronic stress.

Think back to a time when you made headway with your work. What were you doing? And more importantly, *how long* were you doing it for? Maybe the project lasted six months, but **how long were you *fully* engaged in your highest contribution** *on a single day*? We're all living in a collective illusion of productivity.

## Multitasking Is Inefficient

One study showed that two-thirds of workers feel they don't have enough time to get all their work done, and 94 percent have at some point felt "overwhelmed by information to the point of incapacitation."[9]

After each interruption, it takes ten to twenty times the length of the interruption to return focus to the previous task. That means that if you take just one minute to respond to a text or check email in the middle of another project, it will take you *ten to twenty minutes* to get back to the original task. Researchers at the Institute of Psychiatry, Psychology, and Neuroscience at King's College London studied 1,100 workers at a British company and found that multitasking with electronic media caused a greater decrease in IQ than smoking marijuana or losing a night's sleep. Another study found that Fortune 500 CEOs averaged only twenty-eight uninterrupted productive minutes a day![10]

The solution for this "always on" dilemma is actually quite simple: we must reclaim a more cyclical pattern by working in a focused, concentrated way with no distractions for discrete periods of time, followed by unmitigated downtime based on our bodies' natural rhythms.

## Harness Your Ideal Rhythm: The Power Hour

Science has discovered that our brain naturally goes through cycles with peaks and valleys. When you fall asleep, you enter REM-cycle sleep after about ninety minutes of non-REM sleep and continue to cycle in this way throughout the night. As it turns out, our brain and body go through similar oscillations, from higher to lower states of alertness, during the day. Our heart alternates between beating and resting, our lungs inhale and exhale. We can maximize our output by honoring these peaks and valleys and integrating relaxation into our days.

Most of us are conditioned to crank it out and ignore our fatigue and boredom. But what if these are actually symptoms that our body is sending to remind us to take a break? What if instead of listening to our inner critics and dismissing these impulses as personal flaws, we treated our fatigue and lack of concentration as important data about ourselves? What if distraction is a sign that your optimal level of focus for a given task has peaked, and it is time to move on or recharge?

I use a simple tool to teach corporate audiences how to work in pulses or cycles. I call it the "Power Hour" and recommend observing two things: (1) how you *feel*, and (2) how much you accomplish on your most meaningful objectives. (No, it isn't a drinking game involving Ping-Pong balls. It's loosely based on the Pomodoro Technique, which was created in the late 1980s by then university student Francesco Cirillo to help him better focus on his studies. He would work in ten-minute increments, using a kitchen timer shaped like a tomato, or *pomodoro* in Italian.)

A Power Hour consists of working in concentrated chunks of time followed by short periods of rest. Begin with twenty-minute intervals and increase from there. This will allow you to harness the optimal performance of your brain and body.

### Power Hour Instructions

1. Make a list of your top three priorities for the day. These are the most meaningful objectives for moving your goals forward.

2. Set a timer for seventy-five minutes to do your Power Hour. (Yes, it actually takes a little more than one hour when you factor in breaks!)

3. Put away *all* distractions. Close out your web browsers, turn off alerts, shut down social media apps, put your phone on silent. The *only* web browser or application you should have open on your computer is what you need to accomplish your number one most important priority.

   • If needed, signal to others, with headphones or even a "Do Not Disturb" sign, that you shouldn't be interrupted.

4. Twenty-Minute Interval: Start with the number one priority on your list and focus on completing it for twenty minutes. If you complete priority number one, move on to number two and then number three, but only work on one priority at a time for twenty minutes.

5. Two-Minute Break: At the end of the twenty minutes, take a two-minute break. Do something unrelated to work. Walk down the hallway and get a glass of water, go to the bathroom, or stand up and stretch.

6. Twenty-Minute Interval: When the two-minute break is up, complete another twenty-minute interval focusing on one of your priorities.

7. Two-Minute Break: When that focused interval is over, take another two-minute break.

8. Twenty-Minute Interval: Complete a third twenty-minute interval, again focusing on your top priority.

9. Ten-to-Fifteen-Minute Break: Do something unrelated to work. Call a friend, go for a short walk, meditate, or lie on the floor listening to music with your legs up the wall.

10. Begin another Power Hour.

I recommend trying the Power Hour first thing in the morning when your willpower is likely the strongest, and your focus is high, although this may depend on your chronotype (whether you're an early bird or night owl).

To truly work in pulses, you must allow your brain to *relax* and completely disconnect from work during your breaks.

I invite you to play around with intervals to see what works best for you. Start with twenty minutes and gradually extend it. You may find you can stretch your focused segments up to ninety minutes. Most people max out around two hours before the brain and body need to disengage. If you pay attention, you'll notice your own cues. Several clients, including leaders at Fortune 100 companies such as Google, have told me *three years* after working with me that they still use the Power Hour every week, and it has been game changing.

### Mindset Shift #4—Reclaiming Leisure and Pursuing Pleasure

To find The Soul Solution, we must be fierce about our boundaries. As I began to intentionally allow myself more time for leisure, inner alarm bells went off in my head: *You're lazy!* my inner critic chided. *You should respond to emails* before *you take a break. You can't just lie around in the middle of the day!*

When you begin carving out time, you may notice your inner critic and protective parts getting *louder* and encouraging what I call "leisure loss" (or internal pressure to decrease pleasure time). Stick to your commitment to downtime!

### Leisure: The Hard Work of Doing Nothing

You must make a conscious effort to *do nothing*. When you try to carve out leisure time, chances are you *will* be tempted to check email, wipe the counters, pick up toys, or run errands. Your conditioning will draw you back to work like a moth to a flame. As my client Ulrika lamented, "When I sit down on the couch to have a moment of leisure, I make notes in my head of what I'll do *after* I sit on the couch, which takes away from the whole purpose!"

You must *notice* and *name* this pattern.

Physically *stop* yourself from doing the laundry or sending that email. Put your phone high up on a shelf so you can't reach it and **stay lying on the couch** as if your life depends on it!

Repeat to yourself, *I am allowing myself to do nothing. This is important for my well-being. I allow myself to relax. This is sacred time. This is safe, and this is very, very good for me. All is well. All is well. All is well. I am exactly where I need to be.*

Having a daily meditation practice can help you calm the mind's tendency to jump straight to the to-do list when you want to relax. Using a mantra or affirmation like the ones above gives your mind something calming to focus on.

For some women, it helps to have a "brain dump" list either in the notes section on your phone or on pen and paper. This is where you list *all* the things you have to do, *not* your to-do list for a single day. It is simply a way to get all those thoughts out of your head, so your brain can feel secure that the tasks won't be forgotten.

Yes, leisure makes you more productive—
but that's not the point!

Because leisure does not have a tangible output, it may seem "inefficient." However, when you allow your mind to wander, it activates the brain's default mode network or DMN, which is crucial for empathy, self-reflection, creativity, and innovation.

Being productive is not really the point! The purpose of leisure is not just to help you be more effective at work but also to *enjoy your life*. Your leisure is intrinsically valuable.

### Your Mom's (or Society's) Relationship with Leisure Is Not Yours

When we peeled back the layers on what stops Ulrika from allowing herself pure leisure time, she shared, "A part of me is like, 'Why should I sit on the couch and relax?' You just don't do that. My mom never just sat down and relaxed, so I probably got that from her."

If any of this sounds familiar, revisit the Source Your Beliefs Tool from chapter 5 and the Belief Reprogramming Tool at the end of this chapter.

With focus and practice, you can reclaim your sense of deservingness when it comes to leisure and pleasure. This is very, very important work.

### Leisure and Human Connection

When we get in hustle mode, living at a busy and frantic pace, we also often forget to connect with the actual human beings in front of us. How many times have you been in a rush at the grocery store and forgotten to really *look* into the eyes of the checkout clerk and ask how they're doing? When we live with tunnel vision, we block off human connection. One important aspect of leisure includes taking time to have conversations.

Recently I went on a run as part of my cycle of working in pulses. When I returned, sweaty and out of breath, our lovely neighbor was outside her house. Part of me automatically thought, *I don't have time to chitchat*, but then I remembered that this is exactly what Celeste Headlee writes about in her book. One reason we are depressed and lonely is because we've sacrificed a natural level of human connection, believing that it's a "waste of time."[11]

Even though I knew that this new, more relaxed approach to life will make me more joyful and more productive, it wasn't easy to force myself to stop working at a frantic pace. But then the most magical thing happened. After chatting for a few minutes, my neighbor invited me to sit on a bench outside her house next to a babbling fountain. She showed me the new seeds and blossoms on one of her trees and told me it's her favorite time of year for that particular tree. Then she showed me a technique her yoga instructor taught her: face one area outside or in your room and really see it, taking in all the details in ways you never have before. We spontaneously decided to do the practice together, staring at a bush outside her front door that neither of us had really taken the time to notice. We found these luscious soft blooms that felt like velvet under our fingertips and I thought, *This is life. This is living. Not rushing straight back to my computer after a run.*

I had gotten so rigid about working in pulses that I was even taking that structure too seriously with no extra cushion for spontaneous enjoyment, leisure, or doing nothing. As you implement the frameworks from this book, the most important thing is to continually check in with *you*. Notice if you are being rigid with some of these new tools and allow yourself space to play, be spontaneous, and trust your impulses from moment to moment.

### Be Persistent about Pleasure

Two simple ways to increase pleasure: (1) savor the gratifying experiences you *already* have in your daily life, and (2) prioritize bringing *additional* pleasure in. In the morning, set an intention to notice existing pleasures and do at least one pleasurable new thing. **Pleasure is already happening**, but we often take it for granted. Be on the lookout for the way the leaves rustle in the breeze outside your window and pause to take pleasure in this calm movement. Instead of being on autopilot, savor the feeling of water cascading down your body in the shower or holding a warm mug in your hand. Slow down enough to enjoy the taste of a delicious meal on your tongue. When your child or pet runs to greet you at the door, see if you can *extend* the good feelings for up to fifteen seconds longer. Close your eyes and soak in the pleasurable sensation.

Make pleasure a priority. Block time on your calendar to do something that brings you pleasure each day. These can be small acts, and yet they have a big impact.

Is there a certain glass you really enjoy drinking out of? Do you get a kick out of mint leaf garnishes and oversized ice cubes? It sounds silly, but I have discovered that when I make "Banana Swirls" for myself and the kids (a smoothie with frozen bananas, dates, coconut milk, cinnamon, and sometimes peanut butter), I get a little jolt of joy from drinking it out of these *particular* fancy brandy glasses from our cupboard. Take small actions to bring yourself pleasure each day. Buy yourself affordable luxuries such as fresh flowers or an expensive bar of chocolate; use the nice napkins or make a beautifully arranged plate of snacks. It will feel silly and self-indulgent. Do it anyway. Do it *because* it feels silly and self-indulgent.

We tend to dismiss or shame ourselves for our pleasure. It's an entire book unto itself, but women, sexuality, and pleasure have been in a tangled knot for centuries. If you deny yourself pleasure, feel guilty when you do something that brings you pleasure, or feel like you need to "earn" the right to pleasure by doing something unpleasant *first*, you are not alone.

Reclaiming your pleasure is part of reclaiming your power.

Believe it or not, listening to what brings you pleasure will also bring you closer to the whispers of your soul. It's all connected. As you give yourself permission to have more pleasure, that satisfaction will trickle into every aspect of your life.

## Implementing Mindset Shifts

Now that you are familiar with these mindset shifts, I recommend choosing one shift that you'll focus on first. See if you can tune in, perhaps placing your hands on your heart or taking two to three deep breaths into your heart center, and then asking yourself, *Hmmm, which of the mindset shifts would be most helpful for me to focus on first?* Allow yourself to be surprised by the answer. It may not be what you expect.

Then come up with at least one action step you will take to put the new mindset into practice.

Unwinding the Success Myth starts with an internal awakening and a commitment to radical responsibility, which you have already begun, followed by turning to *your* inner authority for answers rather than a dysfunctional system. We must all think very much outside the box and outside the norms as they have been defined.

You are part of the solution. Maybe choosing to take a slight pay cut to work for a large organization in whose values and family-friendly policies you are more aligned is the radical move. Maybe you'll become an activist, help change policies within your organization, or join the gig economy so you can own your schedule and model more sustainable success for others. My goal is to give you a road map for reclaiming your truth so that you can find your authentic voice, take a stand for your values, and assume your rightful and joyful place on the world's stage.

While it's helpful to study other people's journeys, your greatest contribution will no doubt come from finding your *own* path.

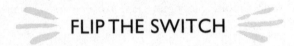

# FLIP THE SWITCH

## Belief Reprogramming Tool

Belief reprogramming occurs when you intentionally decide to cultivate new beliefs in order to create different results in your life. Here are ten simple steps to reprogram old beliefs:

1. List old beliefs.

2. Choose one to focus on.

3. Where do you think this belief comes from? (You may have already done this with the Source Your Beliefs Tool in chapter 5.)

4. How has this belief served you? Journal.

5. How has this belief limited you? Journal.

6. How do you *feel* when you operate in that way? What is the cost of operating in that way? What might be possible if you were free from that? Journal.

7. List the new belief(s) you'd like instead.

8. What evidence or reasoning do you have that shows this new belief is as true or truer than the old belief? Journal.

9. What's your first warning sign that you're operating in the old belief? Are you tense in your body? Spinning in your mind?

10. Practice noticing your warning sign and then ask, *What's a choice I can make from the new belief in this moment?*[12]

# Hustle-to-Flow Shift Moves (Mindset Shift #2)

Here are some quick exercises to move you from hustle to flow. First, get curious and ask yourself, *Hmmm . . . what puts me into a state of flow? What are my "tell" signs when I'm caught up in hustle?*

Get to know your body's signs so you can easily recognize when you're in hustle or flow. Pause throughout the day to ask yourself, *Am I in hustle or flow right now? How do I feel?* When you observe yourself in hustle, make a conscious choice to move into flow. The first step is you must *notice* when you are in hustle and then make a change to intentionally move toward flow.

### Solution: PAUSE Mid-Hustle

Ask yourself, *How am I* **feeling***? What is my body posture? What's going on with work, home, relationships? What beliefs or fears are running the show? What is the voice in my head saying?*

### Hit the RESET Button

Give yourself permission to get back into the flow mindset by doing one small thing (options listed below).

### Suggested Flow Shift Moves

- Move your body. (Example: set a timer for one to ten minutes and move your body however it wants to move.)

- Change your posture to be more expansive.
  (Example: Stand with your arms reaching out wide,
  back arched, head tilted toward the sky; or move
  your arms like seaweed flowing with the current.)

- Takes three deep breaths.

- Meditate.

- Walk the dog.

- Spend time in nature.

- Listen to music.

- Dance to music.

- Exercise or do something to increase your heart rate.

- Smell essential oils.

- Repeat an affirmation: "I am safe. I am loved. All is well."

- Repeat a commitment statement: "I commit to
  joyfully expanding in flow every single day and
  inspiring those around me to do the same."

Create your own personal list of hustle-to-flow shift moves
that you can deploy anytime you notice yourself in hustle. Put
this list somewhere you can easily see it—on a sticky note on
your computer or bathroom mirror, for example. Read it daily.

## Soul Symbol

## Resolution of Duality

This symbol invites you to challenge your sense of separate self, let go of duality ("right" and "wrong," "us" and "them") and question any belief systems or thoughts that limit you. Recognize how your individual issues are connected to the whole, and as you resolve and transform, you contribute to collective upliftment. Breathe in and out deeply while gazing at this symbol and say to yourself: *I am the resolution of duality.*

We are all connected, we are all one.

I say yes to a multidimensional perspective that is beyond "good" and "bad."

# PERMISSION TO BE A SLACKER

**M**any years ago, one woman shared a story that really struck me: Her husband was in charge of picking up their son from daycare and hadn't realized that the schedule had changed. He told his wife over dinner that night that he'd accidentally arrived forty-five minutes early for pickup. "So, what did you do for those forty-five minutes?" she asked. "I got a beer," he replied. "You got a beer?" she responded incredulously. "At three o'clock in the afternoon! Before picking our son up from daycare?!"

"Yup," he answered.

As she relayed this story, every single woman in the room shook her head and sighed audibly. "What would you have done with forty-five minutes to spare?" I asked. "What would *any woman* have done?"

Their answers varied in specifics, but all had the same taking-care-of-business theme:

- Do work in my car.
- Buy diapers or household stuff online.
- Go grocery shopping.
- Make calls, schedule appointments.
- Run an errand nearby.

Every mom in that room said it would never have crossed her mind to get a beer (or even a pedicure!) if she had extra time. She would do something *productive*.

This woman realized that instead of judging her husband, she wanted to be more like him! What if instead of judging others, we began questioning ourselves (with compassion) and asking, *Why am I* not *taking that time to relax by myself?* In a culture that tells women to sacrifice our needs and be all things to all people, it's not surprising we are not taking time for ourselves. Instead of blaming or shaming yourself, focus your energy on *reprogramming* yourself from the toxic messaging about what you "should" do.

Once you've recognized the temptation to overwork, overdo, and over-commit, it takes courage and commitment to take your foot off the gas. If you're an ambitious woman, this will not be easy at first. If you live in the modern, fast-paced world and not under a rock, this will not be easy. It's surprisingly difficult to allow yourself to *do less*, to stop fixing everything and everyone, to drop the to-do list like a hot potato and lounge around like a couch potato instead. Your very identity will be shaken to its core, and that's okay. In fact, that's good. It means the unraveling has begun.

A big part of making The Soul Solution work is learning how to surrender and trust that the universe has your back. Sometimes the best thing to "do" is nothing. Doing nothing, like doing something pleasurable, can actually be quite productive when you are in flow. For example, I got a large crack in my front windshield that I decided not to repair until ski season was over in three months. Just as the snow started melting and I prepared to swap my ski boots for flip-flops, the Subaru dealership called to schedule the last *free* tune-up on my warranty. Because I'd slacked, I got to do *both* the windshield repair and the tune-up in a single visit, saving me an hour of driving and lots of unnecessary inconvenience and appointment making. All that energy was saved thanks to inaction.

It may seem counterintuitive, but often in life you receive more in doing less. It's not easy—after all, you're coming up against a lifetime of programming as you attempt to *achieve nonachievement*. At times, looking at my cracked windshield was like not scratching an itch. It was hard to do nothing because it actually takes discipline to be a slacker. When you are used to fixing every problem, being a slacker goes against every fiber of your being. But slowly, over time, you can strengthen this muscle. (If the word *slacker* is triggering for you, instead focus on the phrase "Do less to *be* more.")

You can choose to nourish yourself, reclaim your time, and do less, slowly. As you do, you'll realize that you're cultivating stillness and clarity from within. This is big, important, and difficult work. In fact, I would argue this is the most important work we can do. We're conditioned to fit into our culture's action-oriented, go-go-go mold, but our bodies and emotions are crying, "Mercy!" Leaning into your inner slacker is one major way to mitigate that burnout.

So, while your old beliefs, coupled with "human-giver syndrome" and cultural messaging, can make doing less hard, you have the ability to shift this internal patterning. When you come together with other women (and men!) who are creating new models of success and leadership, you can begin to craft a new narrative. As more women shift their patterning, we'll change the broader cultural narrative, making it easier for future women to do less *and* have bold, ambitious visions for their lives. So, the next time you're lying on your couch in the middle of the day watching *Real Housewives* and your partner walks into the room with a raised eyebrow, simply say, "Honey, this is a feminist issue. I'm helping unchain future generations of women as we speak. This is vital work." And pop a bonbon in your mouth for emphasis.

In all seriousness, giving yourself permission to do less so you can *be* more is crucial to meeting your greatest potential and feeling sane and satisfied.

## You Are Doing More Than You (Ever) Give Yourself Credit For

The other week, I had lunch with a woman who shared that she had a new business idea but wasn't actively pursuing it. This woman has a big job, two kids, and started a networking group for women CFOs on the side, just for fun. She's doing *a lot* already. After bemoaning how she hadn't done *anything* with this new concept, as we left the restaurant, she casually mentioned that she *had* worked with a brand strategist on the name, logo, and mission statement.

Her dismissal of her own efforts astounded me. This is a common pattern among women. We're doing an incredible amount at work and at home, yet we refuse to give ourselves credit. It's not surprising since our contributions have been trivialized for centuries. I do this myself *all the time*. But if you want to escape the busy trap and learn to do less, it helps to recognize all the ways you're already doing *a lot*.

One way to feel more alert to your daily accomplishments is to begin cultivating satisfaction in small moments. For example, by taking a couple breaths to feel a true sense of *satisfaction* after simply sending an email or wiping crumbs off your kitchen counter, you'll begin to alter your frenzied daily existence and start appreciating what you've accomplished.

I find it helpful to repeat these phrases to myself whenever I notice I'm falling into that "not doing enough" trap:

> *I am exactly where I need to be.*
>
> *I am exactly where I need to be.*
>
> *I am exactly where I need to be.*
>
> *All is well.*
>
> *All is well.*
>
> *All is well.*

Phew! I certainly feel calmer after reading those words. You may want to write these phrases in your Soul Solution Journal and return to them when you feel overwhelmed.

## You Are More Tired Than You Realize

When you slow down and take ten minutes to do *nothing*, chances are you'll discover that you're bone-tired. When all the distractions and tasks get put aside, you're left with your true state stripped bare. Most women I know are deeply exhausted.

At every meditation retreat I've been on, for the first few days, participants consistently nod off during meditation. Glancing surreptitiously around the hall, I see participants' bodies begin to droop and heads loll on shoulders. Before I know it, a few folks are overtly *snoring*! According to the retreat teachers, this is a common occurrence when people slow down. Their bodies are finally able to signal their exhaustion.

If you make it a practice to begin taking ten minutes a day to *do nothing*, you may find that you are too tired to do, well, anything. Maybe you don't even want to read a novel or a magazine. You just want to collapse on the couch. That's okay! You don't have to *earn* this time by doing something beforehand, and you don't have to *justify* it with some tangible output. Just be.

Another potential pitfall is getting overly ambitious about using the time you've set aside to do nothing. Some women think, *Oh, I'll read that fun TMZ article on my phone while I lie here,* but then they get sucked into checking email or go into compare-despair scrolling through social media. Or they choose to read a book that's more work than pleasure. This is why you must DO NOTHING.

Remember when you were a child and spent time just lying in the grass, gazing at the clouds? That's the vibe. Here are some slacking ideas:

- Lie on the couch for ten minutes.

- Lie on the floor with your legs up the wall for ten minutes (yoga pose that rejuvenates you).

- Lie in the sun outside for ten minutes.

- Listen to relaxing music for ten minutes while lying on the floor or reclining in a comfy chair.

- Gaze at the play of light and shadow through a window or on a surface inside.

This stuff is so basic it seems obvious. Yet I still struggle to take the time and space I need. **Simple is not the same as easy.** I cannot overstate how much women need rest and renewal these days. We can all benefit from doing less to *be* more.

## Protected Time Signals Power

As you attempt to do less, you'll meet with inner resistance. Let's address some of the major beliefs and old programming that might obscure your Soul Solution. It starts with time.

Historically, a woman's job was to protect men's time from interruption. Think of the "good" secretary or wife who acted as gatekeeper so that the man could relax in peace with his thoughts (hello Don Draper). As the journalist Brigid Schulte notes in her book *Overwhelmed,* the sociologist Christena Nippert-Eng documented how "women's time has historically been subjected to unpredictable interruptions, while men's ability to experience blocks of unbroken time has been protected."[1]

According to Nippert-Eng, to be interrupted
is to exist in a "state of dishonor."

As Eve Rodsky, author of *Fair Play*, says, "Society views women's time as infinite, like sand, and it views men's time as finite, like diamonds." Implicit in the notion of human givers versus human beings is that there's almost an expectation that women's time can and will be trampled on by the demands of others. This is not okay. Often this is not from any intentional ill will. It's an ingrained absence of boundaries and unspoken expectations, resulting from a kind of trickle-down patriarchy (I just coined that term). When we respond to interruptions by offering our help and availability, we encourage more intrusions on our time. Go to any child's birthday party and watch how many times the mothers are interrupted mid-conversation compared to the fathers. It's astounding, even among dual-income couples who share child-rearing responsibilities equally. Think of your team at work: How comfortable are you interrupting someone who is more junior than you versus interrupting your boss? Your question had better be good if you are interrupting someone "important," right? In meetings, women—of which there are fewer in the room already—are interrupted far more often than men and are less likely to be given credit when we do share our ideas.[2] Can you see how more frequent interruptions of women demonstrate an implicit power differential at home and at work? Our time is more fragmented as a result. The simple truth is that other people will continue trampling on your time until you put up a gosh darn fence.

Take a moment to pause and get curious: *Hmmm, where do I give up my uninterrupted time the most?*

Perhaps things have gotten really unbalanced on the home front after having kids. Or maybe you have people on your team at work who constantly ask you to solve their problems for them. Or maybe you made some obligatory commitment that's sucking up your time. **Your time and attention are your *most* valuable resources—don't squander them.** Remember that people will always try to commandeer your time. You get to choose— and enforce—where to set boundaries.

> ## *Quick Soul Tip*
>
> Answer this question in your Soul Solution Journal: **Hmmm, how can I carve out more uninterrupted time?**
>
> One action step I can take to reclaim my time (and therefore my power) this week is:
>
> What:
>
> By When:

## A Room of One's Own: S P A C E

I've worked from home for almost ten years, and for the most part, it's been a good experience. During COVID-19, suddenly our house became a *lot* more crowded. My husband was also working from home, and our kids were both home (which involved our daughter doing online school from her bedroom). Aside from the constant interruptions about snacks, computer and Zoom snafus, and ever-shifting logistics, the whole energy felt different. One day, late in the pandemic, my in-laws took the kids for the whole day. My husband decided to go on a walk while taking a work call. Suddenly I had the entire house *all to myself* for the first time in months. It was *magical*.

I meditated, savoring the absolute stillness around me. That quickly escalated to chanting and dancing around my office to Beyoncé while checking out my reflection in this sacred geometry mirror. I felt sexy, alive, energized, and free. I felt like *me*. After this little musical outburst, I eagerly sat down at my desk to write. Everything felt better. Juicier. More spacious. I hadn't realized how divided my attention was, with all of us in the house together. Unencumbered by other people's needs and moods, qualities that I didn't even realize I'd been repressing surfaced.

The twentieth-century writer Virginia Woolf was on to something big with *A Room of One's Own*. In the book, Woolf argued that there were fewer "great" women writers not because women were creatively or intellectually inferior to men (a common prejudice at the time) but because "male-dominated society had systematically prevented women from having the educational opportunities, private spaces and economic independence to produce great art."[3] It is of vital importance that women reclaim our private, alone space if we hope to fulfill our greatest potential. It's too easy to be waylaid by other people's agendas and opinions. Kids, colleagues at work, and partners at home will impinge on your space unless you make it a sacred priority.

Something profound and magical happens when you spend time alone. It's one of the greatest gifts you can give yourself. When we go through major transitions—whether a change, a loss, or a major societal shift—we need **even more alone time** to ask the bigger questions. That's the only way to truly discover if you like the company you're keeping, and, if you don't, what you want or need to change it.

Historically, women have not been *given* space; we've had to take it. In public, we literally take up less space, assuming submissive body postures despite the "manspreading" to our right and left. People will sit next to a woman rather than a man on an airplane because they know the woman will probably take up less space. If we want to empower ourselves to create lives of meaning, purpose, joy, and impact, we must start to take up more space. As you begin to take space to be with yourself, you'll more fully reside in your body, heart, and soul. This will embolden you to begin taking up more space in the public sphere as well. Yet many of us still struggle to take this space. We don't make it a priority. Why, again, is it so hard for us to do something we know will benefit us tremendously?

Three years ago, I had a vivid dream that inspired me to write this book. In it, I felt deeply called to go to Kauai—alone. But this felt too indulgent. I had two small kids, an exhausted husband, and a business to run. Who was I to go on some elaborate vacation *by myself?* I couldn't justify that much pleasure, so I compromised and tacked on a quick trip to Kauai before meeting my family in nearby Maui.

Plagued by guilt, I succumbed to "leisure loss" and shortened the trip even more and then bought a seat on the latest possible flight, effectively shrinking the trip to only two days. The trip also triggered discomfort because I'd not spent that much time alone in years. It felt selfish and indulgent but also scary to just be with myself.

Yet when I woke up that first morning in Kauai and realized I had an entire day to do *whatever I pleased*, I felt so free and *exhilarated*. Afterward, I remember thinking, *I found myself again.*

You'll probably feel guilty and inclined to shrink the space you intend to take. Notice that tendency and see if you can stretch yourself to take a little more space instead.

## Daily Space

For proper personal nourishment, you must take space for yourself every single day. Every. Single. Day. This will feel impossible and uncomfortable at first. Don't worry! Take baby steps. I recommend choosing one or two sacred spaces either inside your home, in your backyard, or within a convenient ten-minute walk or drive from your house.

Notice if you prefer to be seated or lying down or to be moving your body for alone time. This may change day to day. Check in with your body.

## Bigger Space

Sometimes you need to be alone in a bigger space. This might mean going away for a longer period of time on a retreat or finding a more spacious container, such as nature.

Like so many women, I struggled with postpartum hormone imbalance, isolation, and extreme exhaustion after my daughter was born and my husband returned to work. After about a year, still feeling at sea, I signed up for a silent meditation retreat. In the midst of it, as a tidal wave of anger, sadness, and shame washed over me, I found myself wanting to scream. I confided in one of the teachers, who suggested I do just that: leave the hall, walk into the hills, and release. The next day, I took his advice and went walking. Before long, sadness rocked my body. Pausing at a tree, I desperately grasped onto one of its branches with both hands. I cried, and let loose a primal scream so loud it left me hoarse. Then another and another until my screams turned to laughter. Once calm, I bowed my head in thanks to nature for being so big that she could hold *everything*.

Nature is the biggest container and the most sacred space, which is why it can feel so deeply nourishing to take space alone there.

## Get Curious: How Can You Take Bigger Space?

Ask yourself, *Hmmm, in what ways am I craving a bigger space right now?* Maybe the idea of taking a solo retreat at a hotel for one or two nights lights you up, or maybe you're craving a getaway with a girlfriend. Notice what compels you. There is no right or wrong answer, just questions and the answer that feels right to you.

## Recurring Space

Years ago, someone raised their hand on the last day of a retreat and asked, "How do we maintain this inner stillness when we go back into the 'real world'?"

The teacher replied, "Book your next retreat." Everyone chuckled. But he wasn't joking. It's important to have contemplative time scheduled on your calendar, otherwise the daily demands of life can get in the way.

For the past four years, I've been a member of a Divinity Circle with eight other women that meets one Sunday of every month. While this isn't strictly alone time, it's in service to myself. I feel so seen by these women that it nourishes my soul on the deepest level. Having these recurring gatherings on my calendar makes it easier to follow through. When I first joined, I wasn't sure how my family would cope with my absence. Now I can't imagine *not* doing it. By booking a babysitter some Sundays and encouraging my husband to go hike or hit golf balls, he gets to take space as well. Now my husband and kids *expect* me to go and know I always return happier and able to show up more fully as the mom, wife, and businesswoman I want to be.

What comes to mind for you? What do you need? Consider scheduling some sort of recurring time alone or nourishing time with others (who ask nothing of you). You'll find the guilt and resistance diminish as you get used to having this on your calendar. Plus, you save time and energy by avoiding rescheduling every time. The logistics of that alone can feel too exhausting to manage and can be the hurdle that stops you from taking the space you need. When you commit to something in advance, as the day approaches, you don't have to do the work of justifying it or planning it. Try it for yourself and see:

> I commit to taking space to _____ (be alone/be
> with X friend/go on a meditation retreat/etc.) every
> _____ (two weeks/one month/six months/year).

If you take longer space (a night away), another important benefit you'll likely enjoy is a good night's sleep! Any space you take will allow you more rest, which is a vital part of The Soul Solution.

As you take more time and space for yourself, you'll notice an insidious belief crop up that you should *earn* your down time. But the to-do list is never-ending, so we never quite manage to earn the break we need. Instead, what if you were to dismantle this unhelpful belief and cultivate the idea that you **deserve** to take a break, no matter what? You are already worthy of rest and renewal.

> There is no prerequisite of exhaustion to
> get into the club of nourishment.

## Lower the Bar: The Most Mediocre Mom

In addition to taking space for yourself, another strategy for strengthening your slacker muscles is to lower your self-imposed expectations.

My friend Celina knew she wanted to be the CEO of a large company, but she didn't realize how challenging it would be for her to abdicate control of things on the home front in order to thrive at work. She had plenty of experience delegating, but she felt like she wasn't living up to her own *internal* expectations. She realized she needed to lower the bar. So, Celina made being the "most mediocre mom" her new objective, which meant shifts such as her husband cooking or ordering takeout instead of homemade meals when she was on deadline. She reframed the impossible standards that were holding her back.

Notice when you're chaining yourself to an unnecessarily high ideal and see if you can lower the bar. Let go of the pressure you feel to be perfect and instead embrace messy, real life. Begin by noticing all the ways you are overdoing it at work and at home. Do you really need to make homemade cupcakes for the birthday party? Or a full Powerpoint slide deck for that meeting? Start to shift the belief that success must require a massive effort. Ask yourself, *What if I prepare less for that presentation? What if I let the house be messy, don't bother curling my hair, and don't take the kids to that faraway activity?*

## Radical New Solution: Underprepare (Sometimes)

The urge to overprepare is real. I get it. Dotting your i's and crossing your t's can give you a sense of control. It probably got you to where you are today. But it may also be contributing to your exhaustion and isn't as necessary as you've come to believe. Thank the part of you that knows how to work really hard and be thorough, then tell her she's overdue for a vacation, and you'll be taking over while she's out of the office.

When I worked in private equity, I sat on the board of a skincare company. Years later, when I began offering leadership development sessions, the CEO hired me to work with his team. After my keynote presentation, I asked him conversationally what he saw as the biggest barriers for women leaders within his organization. Using one particular executive as an example, he said that female employees tend to run themselves ragged, which isn't sustainable, especially once kids are in the picture. "I told her to work less hard," he said. "Frankly, her B-quality work is the equivalent of an A from any of the other sales managers, but she is having a hard time letting herself do 80 percent." She is not alone.

For example, many women who work "part-time" actually work full-time hours but are only partially compensated because they're not fierce with their boundaries. You have to be okay not giving your all to everything that crosses your desk if you want to keep your sanity intact. As women, one of the ways we can empower ourselves is to stop taking responsibility for everyone else's problems. **We are not the fixers of the world.** If you give too much of yourself, you'll burn out. And then the world won't benefit from your bright light.

Take a moment to think of something that has been frustrating or tiring you. Take a step back and ask yourself, *How am I making this harder than it needs to be? How can I do less?*

See if you can allow things to be just 5 percent easier.

If you were to prepare for that presentation 5 percent less, or clean the house 5 percent less, what might that be like?

Hint: When you are in doubt, remember your core values from chapter 5 and what really *matters* to you. Focus on getting A's in those areas and let the rest go.

Begin to notice some of the menial tasks you take on that might be preventing you from making higher-level contributions. Have a meeting with your manager or coworkers at work and your loved ones at home to request a redistribution of labor. Feeling overwhelmed, I finally sat my husband down and tearfully said, "I need your help. **I can't seem to stop myself from doing all this menial household work. Can you help me?**" When I got vulnerable and asked for his support, he was more than willing to step up. The tactics I *had* been using—sighing dramatically, grumbling under my breath, and stewing in resentment or lashing out with curt demands—hadn't evoked the same sympathy. (Shocking, right?) See if you can have a more **explicit conversation** with those around you to change these patterns.

## Find Role Models Who Are Slackers Too

Once, I noticed a sign that read "Working Girls Cafe." It pictured a woman holding a briefcase in one hand and coffee in the other, *running* in heels. I stopped in my tracks to stare, as I realized, *This is the projection about what it means to be a working woman! No wonder we're all so exhausted. I can't even imagine a sign with a man running without assuming there must be a building on fire, and yet this image of a woman scrambling from one place to another appears so natural and normal to me. This is* messed *up!*

When it comes to bucking societal norms and giving yourself permission to slack, it's extremely useful to find role models who take leisure time, show up not always perfectly coiffed and prepared, and are comfortable as their messy, imperfect selves in front of others. Seek out women who are satisfied *and* successful *and* okay with not doing it all and with taking time for themselves. When you surround yourself with women who will walk with you side by side on this path of imperfection, the journey becomes that much easier.

Remember, simple is not the same as easy.

While the concepts in this chapter appear simple and straightforward, I lovingly challenge you to take an honest look at your life and whether you are able to take the time and space you need to adequately nourish yourself. If the answer is no, see if you can begin to stretch your slacker muscles by taking just five to ten minutes more a day to yourself. Spending time alone is the quickest way to recharge and reconnect with your True Self. When you spend time alone, you are not only recharging your energy but also reconnecting with your inner power source. This is your source of wisdom and guidance. This is how you come back home to yourself. This is how you access The Soul Solution. It is hard to come home to the *real* you with other people in the room. When you make it a priority to get the time and space you need, you will be amazed at the impact.

# FLIP THE SWITCH

Here are some commonly held beliefs about time, space, and productivity that women struggle with and antidote actions for each to help you reach The Soul Solution:

**Old Belief:** My time is not my own. There is never enough time.

**New Belief:** There is always time for what matters most. I choose how to spend my time. I take 100 percent responsibility for my relationship with time.

**Action:** Carve out time to do something that pleases you in the next week.

**Old Belief:** I must overprepare, strive for perfection.

**New Belief:** I can lower the bar, prepare less. I choose to do less to *be* more. It's okay to score a B-.

**Action:** Do 5 percent less.

**Old Belief:** I have to earn the right to rest. I have to *justify* my leisure.

**New Belief:** Rest and renewal are my birthright.

**Action:** Begin to notice when you're not allowing yourself to rest and recharge until you earn it. Notice how you can never really "earn" it, no matter what you do. Take five to ten minutes to do nothing.

Cultivate a sense of deservingness with these affirmations and permission slips:

I deserve to have my needs met.

As I nourish myself, I am able to show up more fully for others.

Being alive qualifies me to take time and space for myself.

I joyfully take the time and space I need.

**Old Belief:** Other people will suffer if I take time or space to myself. It's selfish and will hurt others.

**New Belief:** When I take space for myself, everyone benefits (including me).

**Action:** Take ten minutes alone. Carve out a longer space in the next month.

**Taking care of needs is not a zero-sum game.** Nourishing yourself is the best way you can nourish others. Not only will you have more to give but you will also encourage others to figure out their own solutions rather than relying on you.

## Slacker Permission Slips

If you're still struggling to connect with your inner slacker, revisit the permission slip exercise from chapter 8:

I give (first name, last name) permission to not do it all.

I give (first name, last name) permission to be a slacker.

Read that permission slip every morning and throughout the day whenever you remember. This will help begin to rewire your subconscious mind. If you continue to feel stuck, I recommend a private session with Carl Buchheit from NLP Marin (see resources).

## Soul Symbol

### Imix
(pronounced ee'-meesh)

This symbol represents the primordial Mother and your ability to receive nurturance, support, and self-love. Breathe in and out deeply while gazing at this symbol and ask yourself: *What part of me is most in need of nourishment and support right now?*

I trust all will be provided.

I say yes to receiving deep nourishment and support from the Great Mother.

# Chapter 12

# THE UPWARD SPIRAL

ears ago, I had the pleasure of attending a workshop with Russ
Hudson, the coauthor of *The Wisdom of the Enneagram*. On the last
day, one participant raised her hand and expressed her frustration
over grappling with the same problem again and again in her life in different
forms. She couldn't fix this pattern.

"People often complain about having the same issues crop up over and
over again," Hudson said. "What, do you want *new* issues to deal with?" (We
all chortled in embarrassed self-recognition.)

I've observed this repetitive experience countless times in my own life
and with dozens of clients as we worked toward The Soul Solution. I'd be a
very wealthy woman if I had a nickel for every time I realized, *Oh, I'm feeling
criticized by my [husband/self/boss/person with a pulse] right now, but . . . wait!
This is not really about them. It's about how I never felt good enough for my mom!
Ugh! Again?!*

Many women on the path of personal development and soul awakening
express frustration when the same issues or themes continually arise. There's
this fundamental misconception that we should figure everything out once
and for all. But true change manifests in an evolving upward spiral in which
the same issues recur, giving us the opportunity to react in different, more
aware, and more productive ways. Sometimes you'll make quantum leaps
in your own perception of yourself and the world, spiraling you to a higher
level. But that doesn't mean that your issues are forever resolved.

Rather than feeling impatient and frustrated when old issues crop up (which stirs the inner critic), see if you can respond in a wiser and more resourceful way from your new vantage point of consciousness. Remember that you are *not* in the same place you were the last time you faced that issue. Because the *issue* is the same, you may incorrectly assume *you* are the same. This is simply not true.

While seeking a vision, my sister received a message about limitations of the human perspective. She was told that reality is shaped like a spiral. If we think we are on a straight path, it is only because the spiral is so big that we cannot perceive the curve that is bringing us back toward the beginning. So, what if the point was never to get from A to B in a linear fashion but to expand upward in a corkscrew?

What might that mean for how you view your life?

Maybe we need to think in 3D instead of 2D. Imagine a spiral going straight up into the sky, but the size of the circles stays the same. If you were to look down at this corkscrew from above, it might appear that a person on the path was simply walking in circles. But if you looked at the corkscrew from the side, you could see they were constantly progressing upward. What if that is the pattern of your entire life?

Remember Tanisha, who did a lot of inner work in preparation for quitting her family business? Well, she had what might have appeared to be "false starts" along the way. When Tanisha first decided she no longer wanted to run the family business, she began exploring a more tangential transition: she planned to sell her father's firm to a larger company and then act as the COO, working for their CEO instead of her father. After months of negotiations, the deal blew up at the eleventh hour. Tanisha was in shock. She thought it was the right next step, but the other CEO showed his true colors as things degenerated. After a few more failed attempts at determining her next move, she took on additional board roles related to diversity and inclusion initiatives with other organizations. As the Black Lives Matter movement gained momentum, Tanisha gained clarity on the role she wanted to play as an ambassador of light, speaking across differences. In the end, Tanisha felt grateful she had not jumped too quickly into the next thing. She had been spiraling upward, closer and closer to her unique genius and her soul's guidance all along. What felt like failed attempts had brought her closer to her truth.

You are not alone, dear reader, if you find yourself dealing with false starts, perceived failures, or reemergent issues. It's crucial to cultivate self-compassion and trust your own process. This is especially true if you are an overachiever who tends to be hard on yourself. Regressions are completely normal—old patterns showing up to remind you how far you have come.

Remember:

You are exactly where you need to be.

You are exactly where you need to be.

You are exactly where you need to be.

All is well.

All is well.

All is well.

## Permission to Ask for Even More
## (and Permission to Change Your Order)

When I got clarity on what I wanted to do after quitting my job in finance, I thought I had it all figured out. I was on this new path, and I was on fire. Until I wasn't. Seven years later, I cofounded another business only to discover that my cofounder and I had different visions. We ended up dissolving our partnership and the LLC.

Now what?

Feeling deeply discouraged and adrift, I took myself to one of my favorite sacred spaces at a wellness spot called Cavallo Point with nothing but a journal, pen, and the book *Designing Your Life*. On the way, I set a new intention: "Universe, give me clarity and guidance on what I'm supposed to do next. What new program, online course, or offering should I focus on now?"

With visions of a dip in the heated pool, I changed and stepped outside, dropping my stuff on a nearby lounge chair. With surprise, I noticed **the exact same book** I had brought sitting on the empty chair beside mine! Soon, the book's owner returned. I held up my copy, she laughed, and we began chatting.

It turned out that she was a lawyer who had taken time off to raise her three children. Now she was ready to reenter the workforce. There was just one problem: she didn't want to be a lawyer anymore. We had a deep conversation about finding your purpose and gaining clarity on what matters to you.

At the end of the afternoon, she said, "I want to work with you. Do you have a program for women like me?" I gasped aloud at the universe's brashness.

I had arrived, exasperated and humbled because I'd assumed finding myself was a one-shot deal—*Thanks for all the guidance, Universe, I can take it from here.* Ha! What a naive little bunny I was. Finding yourself is never one and done. *You* are always evolving, dear friend. There is no end destination.

I wish I had understood the spiraling nature of my own evolution, so I could have been less confused, judgmental, and harsh with myself at the time. Now I see that we are always in the process of expanding, and it's our divine right to keep asking for more. More joy, more creativity, more ease, more abundance, more satisfaction. More of whatever we would like. This does not make us greedy, flighty, or flawed. This is how we fulfill our soul's purpose, by continually coming into alignment with who we are *now* (which is different from who we were ten years ago or even ten minutes ago), hearing the whispers of what's arising *now* and saying yes to those current desires.

As the saying goes, the biggest breakdowns come before the best breakthroughs. My experience of getting lost (again) was humbling but also incredibly validating. The wild thing that happened when I let go of the business I had cofounded is that all the same tools, strategies, and approaches I had used to find myself when I first quit my finance job worked again!

I also used The Soul Solution when I was navigating major transitions after the birth of each of my children. It *always* works because it's a process that teaches you how to come home to the *real* you.

## Being in the Hallway

So many of the women (and men!) I've advised were confronting a crossroads in their lives. During these times, it's important—and difficult—to cultivate trust, allowance, and surrender.

This second big transition at work started with me feeling creatively stagnant. I could tell something new wanted to come through me. My business partner was moving; I was seven months pregnant. I felt like I was standing on shifting sands, ready to discard some old ways of being but not yet on new solid ground. Ronnie Kaye, the author of *Spinning Straw into Gold* and two-time breast cancer survivor, says:

> In life when one door closes, another always
> opens, but the hallways are a bitch.

I love this line. It's funny but also profound. Being stuck in the hallway is the hardest part of the journey and is where most of us want to give up. "I have struggled with leaving behind my past success and the person that I was," confided one client, "feeling lost and insecure while searching for my purpose and discovering who I am in this new stage of life."

When we're in the hallway, it's tempting to quickly attach ourselves to the first opportunity that presents itself because we are desperate for a sense of stability. We want to jump through the next door we see just to move past this vulnerable, liminal space. We can't stand the unknown. But if we rush to jump, we miss a crucial step: the opportunity for healing and growth. Most significantly, we may miss the unfolding of our soul's true path.

Sometimes you need to wander the hallway in order to find the door you *really* want to walk through. This is not an easy feat. While you're managing your fears and insecurities, it seems like everyone else wants to know what door you're going through next too. It takes courage to pursue this uncertain step when those around you are continually asking for updates. They're also uncomfortable with the uncertainty and are, often unknowingly, projecting their anxieties onto you, triggering your fears.

We all want to have a plan. We want to know what the next thing is—like *yesterday*! Yet it can't (or shouldn't) be forced. During these periods of upheaval, I've found that we must surrender to the unknown, allow ourselves to be in no-thing, and trust until we find our something. The level of surrender that's required is scary. I'd rather do almost anything else. But I've come to realize that surrendering to the unknown is the most courageous thing we can do. It's also a key step in The Soul Solution.

## Leaping Is Not Always Graceful

Sometimes, to inspire, people invoke the quotation, "She leapt, and her wings appeared." But I feel like it should be more like, "She leapt, desperately flapped her arms in a pitiful imitation of a chicken, shrieked like her hair was on fire, shouted obscenities, scrambled to grab an overgrown limb as she plummeted to certain death, was bloodied and bruised while her only companion, the inner critic, berated her nonstop saying, 'This will never work. You look ridiculous. We're going to die.' She was about to give up and curl into the fetal position, then her wings appeared."

Okay, maybe it's not always that chaotic. I've had moments of pure grace, where I leapt and magic really did appear quickly. But I've also had times where I felt like I was clawing my way toward the magic. No matter what, I can tell you from experience, it's still worth it. The more you leap, the more you build faith in yourself and in your soul's ability to show up for you when you begin showing up for your higher self.

In his book *Greenlights*, the actor Matthew McConaughey shares how he realized his life had become more interesting and richer than the characters he was playing in rom-coms. He wanted to portray more complex characters. There was just one problem: no one was interested in casting him in dramatic roles. He was the shirtless heartthrob jogging on the beach and no one wanted him to climb outside that cute, dimpled box.

So, he made a fierce decision to turn down all rom-coms (no matter how much they paid) and hold out for a part about which he felt passionate. He waited for *three years*.

Eventually he got what he wanted: he was cast in *Dallas Buyers Club*. But first he had to say no to what he *didn't* want. He refused to compromise or do work that didn't light him up.[1] Matthew McConaughey hung out in the hallway *for over three years*, trusting that he would find a door that felt like a "*Hell yes!*"

Lately I've been experimenting with the thought, *What if I only agreed to the work projects, social invitations, and opportunities that feel like a* Hell yes? *What might my life look like if I lived in radical alignment with what feels really good?*

I'm still very much a work in progress, as we all are. Wherever you are on the spectrum, questions like the above will bring you closer to the rich, satisfying, fulfilling life you desire.

## You Are Allowed to Upgrade Desires

Many women I coach feel trapped in old agreements and stale situations. They say, "But I told my boss/husband/friend I would do X, so I *have* to do it." Years ago, at a workshop with Gay and Katie Hendricks, there was a participant who was struggling with a longtime agreement with his partner. He felt obligated to stay the course and honor his prior commitment. I vividly recall Katie saying, "You *can* make a new agreement."

Wait, what?! You can just *make a new agreement*? That was a revelation to me! I thought agreements had to be honored, no matter what. What she helped me understand is that what must be honored is having **clear agreements** and **upholding your current agreements**. But that doesn't preclude you from updating what's no longer working.

Often situations get sticky because, when we want change, instead of making a new agreement, most of us just dishonor the old one. We take the back door out. We self-sabotage or create drama to avoid our commitment. This causes the people around us to feel betrayed and hurt. Instead, if we have upfront conversations about what is and isn't working, we have a better chance of coming to a new agreement.

What matters *most* is that **you are in integrity with yourself**. Being in integrity with yourself means you are being honest about your truth, deeper needs, and desires. If you're in integrity with others, but it comes at the cost of betraying your true needs, you're actually betraying others as well because you are presenting a false self to them. If you're no longer aligned with an agreement, then it's time for a new version. In hindsight, when I felt stagnant in the business I'd cofounded, my feelings of annoyance, resentment, and restriction were all red flags, alerting me to the fact that the current arrangement was no longer workable for me.

Anytime you feel resentful or annoyed, it may be time for a new agreement. If, for example, you agreed to stay home with the kids for a few years, maybe now you're ready to return to work, and you need a new agreement with your spouse about rebalancing contributions to the family. Perhaps you need your spouse to step up more on the home front and allocate a portion of the family budget to your professional development *before* you find your next move. You want to make a clear, updated agreement with your partner about what this might entail.

You may also find that an old desire has morphed into something new. This doesn't mean that you made a mistake. Remember, our desires are always evolving. Give yourself permission to be honest about where you are now and what really excites and energizes you today. It might be different from what made you feel alive yesterday, and that's okay. Sometimes we have to catch up with *who we really are.* Your mind is likely to cling to old stories about what you "think" you want, but your heart and intuition will speak the truth. Listen in a new way, not to the voices in your head but to the feelings in your body.

## Quick Soul Tip

Spend twenty minutes journaling "hot pen" style (stream of consciousness) on these four questions (write nonstop for the full twenty minutes):

How am I *really* doing?

Who do I want to be now?

What would I like?

What do I need to support me in creating and receiving that?

When you let go of a desire that you've outgrown, it creates space for a new desire to come through. Often in order to make room, we have to enter an uncomfortable period of transition—the hallway.

## Surrender, Allow, and Trust

The universe has your back. Always. A simple way to remind yourself of this truth is to change "Things are happening *to* me" to "Things are happening *for* me." Begin to reframe when things are not going how you want. If something you judge as "bad" happens, get curious and ask, *Hmmm, how might this be happening for me?* When you're in a really bad mood, it can be hard to ask this question with genuine curiosity. You may have to reset yourself emotionally first—go on a walk, scream, cry, call a friend, take a nap, and then once you have calmed down, ask yourself again.

What if that confrontation with your boss that led to getting fired was the best thing that ever happened to you? What if it freed you from a toxic environment and gave you space to choose something better?

Years ago, my absolute favorite professor had a disagreement with the administration and ended up leaving her job of almost twenty years. She was distraught. This is not what she had planned for the last decade of her career. It turned out to be a blessing in disguise. Once she left academia, she was able to bring her teachings to an even bigger audience. She founded an organization to teach to a wider audience, and she wrote a book. So, you just never know what is around the bend for you. After all, your beliefs create your reality. If things are not working out in your favor, it's because you're still in the hallway. When you get to the other side, you may very well look back with gratitude.

Even if you don't have all the answers today, can you trust that the process will unfold for you? Can you surrender to the hallway and allow yourself to follow your energetic bread crumbs to the door you're really looking for?

Everyone's path is different.

Only you know what would push the boundaries of what's possible for you. You can play it safe and do what you think everyone else expects or trust yourself and surrender to your deeper truth. It's your call.

> Trust is built over time.
> Allowing is a practice.
> Surrender isn't always easy.

Just remember that it's okay if these things don't come naturally, especially in the beginning. I honor your courage with each moment of soul searching. For those dark moments on the path when you feel alone or scared, please know that you've got this. You are exactly where you need to be. You are exactly where you need to be. You are exactly where you need to be. As the poet Mary Oliver writes:

> One day you finally knew
> What you had to do, and began,
> Though the voices around you
> Kept shouting their bad advice.[2]

## Individuating, Together

One of the challenges of any personal growth journey is that as you change and expand, the people closest to you might feel scared or upset. Whenever you're immersed in learning and growing, and those around you are not, it can lead to distance. As one woman asked, "How do you deal with the fallout as people respond to a changed you? You live a more authentic life, but that's disruptive. Especially for women like us who are people-pleasers." Some friendships or relationships might fall away as you begin to live a life more aligned with your values. This can be uncomfortable and painful. But then new friendships and relationships arrive that are more reflective of who you are today.

There's a way to frame this process to invite people on the journey with you and include them as allies. In my own life, I did a somewhat horrible job with this, essentially telling my husband, "I'm changing, come along or not, but this is happening." My approach did not build trust, safety, or connection. In hindsight, I wish I had sat my husband down and said, "Hey, I really care about our relationship, and I really care about you. And even though it's scary, I'm really wanting to change and do this for me. I can imagine this might be hard or scary for you. How can we move through this together?"

A good approach is to ask your partner or loved ones, "How much do you want to be a part of this? And how can we make sure that as I'm doing this, it doesn't create distance between us?"[3] Get their buy-in and input as you learn and grow. If you've decided to be less of a people-pleaser, the impact on the other person is that they now feel less cared for. They might be wondering, *Do I matter? Am I important? What about me?* It's not an either/or—either I do this for me or I take care of you. The way to frame these conversations is to ask how we can do *both*. Reiterate how much your loved ones mean to you while staying committed to your new path.

## The Upward Spiral in Your Community

We are all connected. When you're feeling energized, alive, fulfilled, calm, happy, and creatively stimulated, you bring that energy to those around you and to the world. When you're cranky, short-tempered, or feeling stagnant, you also carry that energy. As you learn how to take responsibility for creating the life you truly desire and begin to use the tools in this book to discover

The Soul Solution, you'll experience progressive growth and expansion. A natural next step in the journey is to take your individual upward spiral of growth and expand it to the community and others around you.

We are all both teachers and students. If this book has tickled your fancy and strummed the strings of your soul in surprising ways, I guarantee it's because, on some level, you're meant to share and teach this work too. It could be with your partner or kids, or with your colleagues at work, or on a broader scale in your community or the world.

Begin to notice who is coming to you for advice or disclosing their struggles. This will happen with greater frequency as you begin to wake up more fully to and embody your soul's truth. Other people will be attracted by your light and your example. Some of them might want you to fix their problems for them. Resist the temptation to do so. This is not the point. What they *really* want is to discover *their* light, to understand that *they* are their own best authority. You now have the road map to help anyone discover their truth and live it in the world. Please share it. Take anything that has been of value and pass it on to others. This is how we can create a ripple effect of positive change in ourselves and the world at large.

## But What If I'm Not "Qualified"?

When I first began coaching people one on one, I was only three-quarters of the way through my certification. It was a serious responsibility, and I didn't feel qualified. My executive coach helped me peel back the layers of self-doubt when she asked me, "What would it take for you to feel qualified?" and the answer that came out was, "I would need to be the Dalai Lama." Ha! Good luck with that one. She then told me to find people who were three steps behind me as they would be exactly right for me to support. This has proven to be sage advice.

So, even if you aren't sure who you are meant to support, simply find the people who are **three steps behind where you are** on your own journey, or the people you find it easy to talk with and who express curiosity about The Soul Solution. Share this process with them.

Your authenticity is what will uplift and transform others. As you apply the tools and techniques in this book and receive the benefits, you'll be able to speak with clarity about your own process, both what worked and what didn't.

You will naturally attract people who are in some way a match to you—perhaps they struggle with a similar issue or have a complementary desire. These are the people you can most easily support. All you need to do is offer your story, share your truth, and pass along any of the tools and resources that you found helpful. This is how you will create an upward spiral that is bigger than you and that will continue expanding after you are gone.

# FLIP THE SWITCH

## Surrender, Allow, and Trust (S.A.T.) Meditation and Script

(Visit vanessaloder.com/book to access the S.A.T. Guided Meditation.)

There's a force greater than us that is at work in our lives. If you connect with this higher power first thing in the morning, you can begin your day with a deeper intention to surrender, allow, and trust in what life has to offer.

A morning S.A.T. meditation practice will help you to connect with the Divine as you ask, "What would you have me do today? Where would you have me go? What would you have me say, and to whom?"[4]

You'll learn a process to surrender, allow, and trust (S.A.T.) the universe, your higher self, or God to move **in you, as you, and through you**.

As you practice this meditation, you will be more connected to your intuition and better able to accept and surrender to life's circumstances. You'll also cultivate a deeper trust that the universe has your back and that good things are coming your way.

Whenever you find yourself confused, at a crossroads, and longing for clarity, sit still and repeat the following affirmations (you can substitute a different word for *universe* such as *God, higher self, True Self,* or *life force*):

I commit to surrendering, allowing, and trusting the universe to align me with what's in my highest good.

I surrender, allow, and trust the universe to carry me forward on my path.

I surrender, allow, and trust the universe to create what's in my highest good and the highest good of all beings everywhere.

I surrender, allow, and trust the universe to bring me into alignment with my truth.

I surrender, allow, and trust the universe to move in me, as me, through me.

In me, as me, through me.

In me, as me, through me.

In me, as me, through me.

I surrender, allow, and trust the universe to move in me, as me, through me.

I surrender, allow, and trust the universe to move in me, as me, through me.

I surrender, allow, and trust the universe to create in me, as me, through me.

What would you have me do today? *(Pause to let the answer bubble up in your awareness.)*

Where would you have me go? *(Pause to let the answer bubble up in your awareness.)*

What would you have me say, and to whom? *(Pause to let the answer bubble up in your awareness.)*

As you repeat these questions, perhaps someone's face will come to mind, or you'll have an impulse to go somewhere, to call someone. I recommend you follow those impulses.

What would you have me do today? *Pause.*

Where would you have me go? *Pause.*

What would you have me say, and to whom? *Pause.*

I am exactly where I need to be. All is well. I trust in myself and the universe to guide me forward with grace and ease.

Every single day, I expand in love, abundance, creativity, and ease, and I inspire those around me to do the same.

## Soul Symbol

## New Myth

This symbol represents the new myth and shift in consciousness that is happening on the Earth at this time, of which you are an integral part. Breathe in and out deeply while gazing at this symbol and ask yourself: *What is being called forth in this present moment? How can I surrender to love and awaken, moment to moment, to the direction of the greater universal plan?*

I let go of rules, road maps, and restrictions as I trust my greater unfolding.

I say yes to claiming my divine place in the bigger story.

# CONCLUSION

Recently I couldn't sleep. I was handing the first draft of this book to my editor the following day and I felt like I was birthing a baby. I kneeled at my altar in the pitch blackness and lit two candles on either side of me. They burned brighter than anything I had seen in a while. Settling into the quiet, a thought arrived: *This is what it's like when you take space and time alone in stillness; the voice of the soul comes through much easier, similar to how these candles burn brighter in the dark of night than when you light them during the day. The soul is like a flame that never goes out. The background of quiet, like the velvety darkness, allows the flame to appear brighter.*

The whole point of The Soul Solution is to access the True Self who is always present in your core and *know*, in your bones, that *you* are the answer and the solution you seek, now and forever. The Soul Solution teaches you how to be in continual, expansive conversation with your soul and the universe. It is an ever-present, ongoing invitation to be in a dialogue and a dance with your higher self. To trust that the answers to your desires and longings are always revealing themselves to you, one bread crumb at a time. To remember that you are lovable and worthy exactly as you are. To honor yourself and your knowing. You are loved. You are beautiful. You are whole and complete, just as you are, with all your flaws and foibles. You don't need to prove your worthiness or earn your enoughness. You don't need to be fixed.

You are exactly where you need to be.

You are exactly where you need to be.

You are exactly where you need to be.

All is well.

All is well.

All is well.

There is no problem, only a solution. Only new desires, new directions you want to go in, new experiences you want to manifest. Ask yourself,

*What if I am the solution I have been*
*looking for, always and forever?*

The paradox is that the more you accept yourself as you are, the more you change, the more you reach The Soul Solution.

Think back to the intention you set at the very beginning of this journey. What has shifted in relation to your desires? What new commitments or recommitments do you want to make as a result of the experiences you've had?

My intention is to connect with those who want to remember their connection to their soul, to discover and unleash their real power so they can have the impact they long to have in the world. More than anything, I want that for you. I want you to remember that oft-repeated saying that you are a spiritual being having a human experience. And I'm so glad you are here. I'm honored that we have been on this journey together, and I also know that it is just the beginning . . . for both of us.

May you have a deep sense of happiness, well-being, and peace.

May you feel safe and protected, both internally and externally.

May you be healthy and strong, and accept your limitations.

May you be free from suffering and the causes of suffering.

And may you be held in loving-kindness.

May all beings everywhere have a deep sense of happiness, well-being, and peace.

May all beings everywhere feel safe and protected, both internally and externally.

May all beings everywhere be healthy and strong, and accept their limitations.

May all beings everywhere be free from suffering and the causes of suffering.

May all beings everywhere be held in loving-kindness.

If you are scared, confused, and full of self-doubt, you are not alone. If you are still in the hallway, you are not alone. Be extra kind and gentle with yourself in these tenuous times. Find a tribe of women who can remind you that you are not alone and who can help shine a light on your unique gifts. Keep following your energetic bread crumbs to your True North Star; they will guide you toward the best next door for you.

One client suggested I end this book with a "You can do it!" pep talk, but nothing was coming to me. So I sat quietly and asked my heart, *What do I need to say to these women?* And my heart answered, *Tell them to do what you just did. They are their own pep talk.*

Pause right now, place one or both hands on your heart. Take two or three deep breaths and gently ask your heart, *What do I need to know right now?* Whatever you hear, or don't hear, is just right. Let that be good enough. Because you are good enough, just as you are.

You are your own pep talk.
The whispers of your soul are always
here, gently guiding you.

And remember, I'm here, cheering you on through every page of this book! Sending my energy, love, and enthusiasm toward you with each word. See, you just got another little bolt of energy right there. Here's another. And another! And one more! And another, just because! Energy and love are streaming through these words from my heart to yours right now. How's that for a pep talk?! You can do this. You always could. Trust yourself.

Now it's up to you.

## Soul Symbol

## CIB
(pronounced keeb)

This symbol represents trusting your inner voice of knowing and intuition. Breathe in and out deeply while gazing at this symbol and ask yourself, *What is the truth my heart wants me to know right now?*

I open to my inner truth with ease.

I say yes to receiving the inner guidance I seek.

We end where we began, with the same symbol, but we are not in the same place at all. Remember you are always spiraling upward, expanding toward your greatest and truest life.

# ACKNOWLEDGMENTS

Thank you to my husband, Brent, for all your love, support, and belief in me. Thank you for not giving up when things get hard. You said at our wedding that you'd follow me up and down mountains, and as Andy pointed out, you had no idea the next mountain would be a spiritual one! But you still joined me, and for that I am eternally grateful. I love you. For Eva and James, may you know your intrinsic worthiness, follow your heart, honor your energetic bread crumbs, and trust yourselves and your inner truth, always. May you remember that you are each a spiritual being having a human experience and you are unlimited. Eva, I appreciate how eager you were to hear passages of this book and offer useful feedback. James, I appreciate all the giggles, joy, and kisses you brought to me throughout this writing process. May you each achieve all your dreams by being exactly as you are. And for Steve Stringbean, who helps us all remember to laugh and be playful.

To all my clients: This book would not exist without you. I am deeply honored you trusted me with your hearts and stories, which are sacred. Special thanks to Elizabeth for the candid conversations, and to all the other women whose experiences are represented in this book. I hope it does you justice and allows other women to see themselves in you and receive new insights and healing thanks to your gracious sharing.

To my dear early readers: Thank you for taking the time to offer your feedback. Your enthusiasm helped me keep going, and your wisdom and insights left prints throughout this book (bad pun intended). Abigail, Amanda, Anne, Brenda, Diane, Ior, Jen S., Jennifer M., Julia, Katie, Kathy, Keenan, Laura, Liese, Linda, Lisa, Malini, Marjorie, Mary Lynn, Molly, Rosaria, Ruchi, Sarina, Shala, Toni, and Vanessa P.—you all made this book better. Extra big hugs and gratitude to Cory (my original muse!), Lauren, Maura, Karen, and Sarah (editor extraordinaire, please publish your writing soon, you're so gifted!) for making it allll the way through the longest version of this manuscript and being available for my quick "What do you think of this?!" emails (Gemma and Suzanne too!). From my heart to all of yours, thank you.

To all the teachers, mentors, and healers who have helped me awaken and discover a more authentic and soul-based path: Alex Merrin, Brian Weiss, Ainslie MacLeod, Gay and Katie Hendricks, Richard Allen, Janet Orion, Jack Kornfield, Julie Wester, Louise Hay, Kristin Neff, Dolores Cannon, Martha Beck, Kristen Wheeler, Byron Katie, Esther and Jerry Hicks and the teachings of Abraham, Shelley Hodgen, Carl Buchheit, Michelle Masters, Rick Hanson, Danielle Rama Hoffman, Wayne Dyer, and Marta Maria Marraccini.

To the authors who inspired my soul awakening and/or portions of this book and who are not thanked elsewhere: Jack Canfield, Bill Burnett and Dave Evans, Viktor Frankl, Russ Hudson, Danielle LaPorte, Marlo Morgan, Bill Plotkin, Richard Schwartz, Michael Singer, and Mark Wolynn.

Eve Ensler, thank you for your fierce feminine energy and for modeling speaking, writing, and living your deepest (and sexiest!) truth. Liz Gilbert, thank you for giving us all permission to be creative *and* joyful. Elizabeth Lesser, thank you for paving the way as a feminist spiritual seeker. RBG, thank you for your bad-assery.

To my Divinity Circle: Thank you for the heart expanding love, light, cosmic goddess connection, multidimensional beingness, channeling, light language, deep belly laughs, and hilarious Long Island impersonations. Hare Daleva, Hara Darshana, Lee Bee, Premananda Sagara, Ravina Darshan, Sarafina, Shivara Hare-San, and our fabulous ceremony and container holder, Hare Shina—I feel so deeply seen, cherished, and alive in your presence, ladies. You bring out my light and playfulness in a way that inspires me to be more *me* in this world. Thank you. You are all a big part of my Soul Solution. And to Ravdna Shiva for your wisdom and guidance: thank you, thank you, thank you. This book would not be here without you.

To all the friends and colleagues who have supported me on this path: Beth Summers, for your wacky sense of humor, which mirrors mine—I love you (said in a sing-song voice); Megan, I'll always cherish our Hendricks training together and your deep empathy; Tanya, for your ruthless truth-telling and generous spirit; Katia, for all the goddess brunches at Cavallo; Kristen Wheeler, the Native Genius® Method creator, for your enormous heart and unquenchable curiosity, plus navigating how to honor your work and mine with so much love and grace; Sherri Lassila, for your divine feminine presence and joyful, easeful collaboration; the ladies in FLI—Ally, Amy, Bianca, Kristen, Lizzie, Meagan, Mollie, Nikki—thank you for sharing the highs and lows of life; Amy Allebest, you inspire me with your grace, authenticity, and world-changing work (Amy's podcast *Breaking Down Patriarchy* is a must listen); Celina, your understanding and kinship on this wild roller coaster from finance to sacred sexuality has been a balm to my soul ("If only I could be a singer, like Jewel!"); and my BVE crew—especially Alison, Dana, and Vanti—thank you for the walks and talks about this book. To my soul sisters, Alka and Jenny: I cherish our girls' trips that nourish my soul, feed my belly, and expand my bliss, and have loved sharing new discoveries on this soul-based path with you. Our friendship deepened on the mountains in Patagonia and continues on the mountains of daily life, I love you both so much. Thank you to my fellow authors, cheerleaders, and T-Group deep sharers: Carole Robin, mentor extraordinaire!; Andy Dunn, twin-flame troublemaker and fun chaser; and Eduardo Briceno, one of the most kindhearted people I know. I'm grateful to the GSB community for supporting me and this work. (A special shout out to Adnan Chaudry, Devon Greensweig, Mike Henry, Scott Holden, Anna Robinson, and Katie Rottier: thanks for trusting me to bring some of these tools to your high-caliber corporate teams and conferences.) To my corporate clients and friends—especially Kelsey Cooper, Suzanne Davenport, Liz Devlin, Marni Heinz, Marilyn Lin, Denali Lumma, Anne Robie, Amanda Santiago, and Jen Scales: I'm grateful to know leaders like you who want to spread mindfulness and soul-based solutions within your organizations.

Thank you to Kelly Notaras (all transformational nonfiction authors who want to get published should read her book!), Annie Wylde, and the entire team at KN Literary for upleveling this book proposal and helping me find an agent with such ease. Thank you to my agent, Lucinda Halpern, for galvanizing others to get behind this book and moving things forward with your fire and grace. Thank you to Nora Zelevansky for your editing prowess and cutting down my redundancy because I say everything twice. Oh shoot! Just did it again. Thanks to the entire team at Sounds True, including my incredibly talented and hands-on editor Diana Ventimiglia for getting the vision for this book, offering sound guidance, and being so responsive and supportive throughout the process. I deeply appreciate your level of involvement and kind, thoughtful approach. Thank you also to Jade Lascelles, Emily Wichland, and the wonderful publicity team at Sounds True. I can't imagine a better home for this book. I'm grateful to Tami Simon for creating a soul-based publishing house that brings these messages to the world—plus your gravelly voice just rocks and you ask the best interview questions on *Insights at the Edge*. (Everyone should listen to that podcast.) To Oceanna, for graciously supporting us in recreating your beautiful drawings of Mayan symbols; and to Ariel Spilsbury, for your divinely channeled words in *The Mayan Oracle*. To my assistant extraordinaire Robyn Inabnit: I could not run the business so smoothly or successfully without your meticulous care and loving support. Thank you for keeping me on track and making everyone who crosses your path feel special and well taken care of.

Isis, thank you for the dream to begin and the guidance in helping me write this book. May I continue to be a clear channel for ancient wisdom and new, off-planet consciousness. Thank you to all the nonphysical beings who helped me on this path: Archangel Michael, Archangel Gabriel, Quan Yin, Mother Mary, Gaia, The Aurora, St. Germain and the Violet Flame, The Council of Light, The Blue Council, The Rainbow Council, Luke, Leo, the Divine Masculine, the Divine Feminine, and my Spirit Guides acting in my highest good. May I continue to stay open to your guidance, unconditional love, and ongoing support.

To my dear sister Alexa Miller: it's been such a joy to wake up separately, together. I'm grateful for your nonjudgmental empathy, deep (like, really deep) wisdom, gentle insight, healing dream-tending, love, and support. I love you. To my dad: Thank you for the humor you bring to my life (in the form of spontaneous one-liners and sporadic *Calvin and Hobbes* texts), for your vulnerability with your own struggles, and for your loving support. To my mom, Andrea: One of the fiercest women I've ever met, also one of the most fraught and challenging relationships of my life. I'm grateful for your love and all the soul-level lessons on forgiveness and unconditional love. I adore you. Now let's let this karma go, shall we?!

I dedicate this book to my mom, and to all mothers and daughters everywhere. May you heal, may you be free.

## ACKNOWLEDGMENTS

Excerpt from a poem I wrote after my mom transitioned to the spirit world:


My mom and I wasted so many years in judgment and blame,
Without ever realizing it was all a big karmic game.
When she was sick and weak and couldn't walk past her own lawn,
I cried and told her I'd miss her when she was gone.
She smiled and said; "Well, then I know I did a good job,
because when my own mom died, I shed no tears, not a single sob."
She never forgave her own mother for abuse, big and small.
So today I give my mom all my love; my anger and pain I let fall.
I thank her for the lessons from Soul to Soul,
Knowing on a deeper level, we both reached our goal.


I love you mom, thank you for this life.
Thank you for teaching me through your love and our strife.
I'm grateful to you for so many things
And I smile inside each time I wear your gold rings.
Our time together on this Earth was rarely easeful and that's ok,
Because I know deep down our spirits are
meeting in love every single day.


I love you, Mom.

# ADDITIONAL RESOURCES

## vanessaloder.com

The following resources are all available at vanessaloder.com/book:

Befriend Your Feelings Guided Meditation

Deep Sleep Guided Relaxation

Future Self Guided Visualization

Guided Visualization to Boost Immunity, Lower Anxiety, and Promote Healing

Inner Child Meditation

Savor the Good Guided Meditation

Self-Compassion Guided Meditation

Values Tool PDF Handout and Bonus Values Tool Video

## Supplemental Resources

The Native Genius® Method created by Kristen Wheeler: nativegenius.com

Book a private session with Carl Buchheit of NLP Marin: carlbuchheitphd.com

Book a private session with energy healer Shelley Hodgen: intuitiveabilities.com

## Recommended Reading List

As you read the list below, notice if any of the titles give you a little *zing* of energy that could be an energetic bread crumb guiding you to read that particular book!

*Ask and It Is Given* by Esther and Jerry Hicks

*The Big Leap: Conquer Your Hidden Fear and Take Life to the Next Level* by Gay Hendricks

*Designing Your Life: How to Build a Well-Lived, Joyful Life* by Bill Burnett and Dave Evans

*The Desire Map: A Guide to Creating Goals with Soul* by Danielle LaPorte

*The Instruction: Living the Life Your Soul Intended* by Ainslie MacLeod

*It Didn't Start with You: How Inherited Family Trauma Shapes Who We Are and How to End the Cycle* by Mark Wolynn

*Many Lives, Many Masters: The True Story of a Prominent Psychiatrist, His Young Patient, and the Past-Life Therapy That Changed Both Their Lives* by Brian Weiss

*Mutant Message Down Under* by Marlo Morgan

*No Bad Parts: Healing Trauma and Restoring Wholeness with the Internal Family Systems Model* by Richard Schwartz

*Soulcraft: Crossing into the Mysteries of Nature and Psyche* by Bill Plotkin

*StrengthsFinder 2.0* by Tom Rath

*The Success Principles: How to Get from Where You Are to Where You Want to Be* by Jack Canfield and Janet Switzer

*The Surrender Experiment: My Journey into Life's Perfection* by Michael Singer

*The Untethered Soul: The Journey Beyond Yourself* by Michael Singer

*The Wisdom of the Enneagram: The Complete Guide to Psychological and Spiritual Growth for the Nine Personality Types* by Don Richard Riso and Russ Hudson

*You Can Heal Your Life* by Louise Hay

## Recommended List of Soul-Based Poetry

*Anam Cara: A Book of Celtic Wisdom* by John O'Donohue

*Consolations: The Solace, Nourishment and Underlying Meaning of Everyday Words* by David Whyte

*The Essential Rumi*, translated by Coleman Barks

*Everything Is Waiting for You* by David Whyte

*Rilke's Book of Hours: Love Poems to God* by Rainer Maria Rilke, translated by Anita Barrows and Joanna Macy

*A Thousand Mornings: Poems* by Mary Oliver

## Sample Assessments

Order *StrengthsFinder 2.0* and take the assessment. (Reading the book is optional, but you must order the book to get the code for your assessment.) If you've already taken this assessment in the past six to twelve months, no need to do it again.

The Enneagram is a model of the human psyche. You can take a free quiz to determine which of the nine interconnected personality types best describes you and gain valuable insight into how you operate in the world. Teams use the Enneagram to better understand each other as individuals and work more effectively together.

## Soul Step

Join our sisterhood at thesoulsolution.com.

# NOTES

## Introduction

1. Olivia Remes et al., "A Systematic Review of Reviews on the Prevalence of Anxiety Disorders in Adult Populations," *Brain and Behavior* 6, no. 7 (July 2016): e00497, doi.org/10.1002/brb3.497; United Nations, Department of Economic and Social Affairs Statistics, *The World's Women 2020: Trends and Statistics*, accessed April 8, 2021, worlds-women-2020-data-undesa.hub.arcgis.com/.

2. Women Business Collaborative, "8.2% of Fortune 500 CEOs Are Women, According to the 2021 Women CEOs in America Report," Cision, October 14, 2021, prnewswire.com/news-releases/8-2-of-fortune-500-ceos-are-women-according-to-the-2021-women-ceos-in-america-report-301400856.html.

3. LeanIn.org and SurveyMonkey, "Women Are Maxing Out and Burning Out During COVID-19," Lean In, May 7, 2020, leanin.org/article/womens-workload-and-burnout#!.

4. Mary Oliver, "The Summer Day," *New and Selected Poems* (Boston: Beacon Press, 1992), 94.

5. Ariel Spilsbury and Michael Bryner, *The Mayan Oracle: A Galactic Language of Light* (Rochester, VT: Bear & Company, 2011).

## Chapter 1: But I Followed the Rules

1. LeanIn.org and McKinsey & Company, *Women in the Workplace 2019*, Lean In, leanin.org/women-in-the-workplace-report-2019/the-importance-of-equal-opportunity-and-fairness.

2. Dalai Lama, Vancouver Peace Summit 2009, Vancouver, British Columbia (no transcript available).

3. Alexandra Sacks and Catherine Birndorf, *What No One Tells You: A Guide to Your Emotions from Pregnancy to Motherhood* (New York: Simon & Schuster, 2019).

4. Jack Canfield and Janet Switzer, *The Success Principles: How to Get from Where You Are to Where You Want to Be* (New York: HarperCollins, 2005), 157.

5. Sarah Gardner and Dave Albee, "Study Focuses on Strategies for Achieving Goals, Resolutions," press release no. 266, Dominican Scholar, February 1, 2015, scholar.dominican .edu/news-releases/266.

6. Ariel Spilsbury and Michael Bryner, *The Mayan Oracle: A Galactic Language of Light* (Rochester, VT: Bear & Company, 2011), 135.

## Chapter 2: The Whispers of Your Soul

1. "Coaching and Conversation with Tara Mohr," transcript, Tara Mohr, May 16, 2021, taramohr.com/wp-content /uploads/2021/05/Coaching-Conversation-with-Tara-Mohr -May-16-2021.pdf.

2. According to the research of Dr. Fred Luskin of Stanford University, a human being has approximately sixty thousand thoughts per day—and 90 percent of these are repetitive. explorecourses.stanford.edu /instructor/fredl; Christine Comaford, "Got Inner Peace? 5 Ways to Get It NOW," *Forbes*, April 4, 2012, forbes.com /sites/christinecomaford/2012/04/04/got-inner-peace -5-ways-to-get-it-now/?sh=176c405f6672.

3. Bill Plotkin, *Soulcraft: Crossing into the Mysteries of Nature and Psyche* (Novato, CA: New World Library, 2003), 167–68.

## Chapter 3: Your Energetic Bread Crumbs

1. Steve Jobs, "Commencement Address," Stanford University, June 12, 2005, transcript, news.stanford.edu/2005/06/14/jobs-061505/.

2. Tara Sophia Mohr, "Why Women Don't Apply for Jobs Unless They're 100% Qualified," Harvard Business Review, August 25, 2014, hbr.org/2014/08/why-women-dont-apply-for-jobs-unless-theyre-100-qualified.

3. Christine Miserandino, "The Spoon Theory," But You Don't Look Sick, butyoudontlooksick.com/articles/written-by-christine/the-spoon-theory/.

4. The Energy Audit is inspired by the "Good Time Journal," in Bill Burnett and Dave Evans, *Designing Your Life: How to Build a Well-Lived, Joyful Life* (New York: Alfred A. Knopf, 2016), 50–55.

## Chapter 4: Discover Your Superpower

1. "Mixed Up in Space," NASA Science, August 7, 2001, science.nasa.gov/science-news/science-at-nasa/2001/ast07aug_1.

2. Gay Hendricks, *The Big Leap: Conquer Your Hidden Fear and Take Life to the Next Level* (San Francisco: HarperOne, 2010), 120.

3. Peter Flade, Jim Asplund, and Gwen Elliot, "Employees Who Use Their Strengths Outperform Those Who Don't," Gallup, October 8, 2015, gallup.com/workplace/236561/employees-strengths-outperform-don.aspx.

4. Hendricks, *Big Leap*, 120.

5. These insights were inspired by the Native Genius® Method module taught by Kristen Wheeler in my online course *Create Work You Love*.

6. Hendricks, *Big Leap*, 132, 140–41.

7. Hendricks, *Big Leap*, 32.

8. Hendricks, *Big Leap*, 31.

9. Linda Babcock et al., "Gender Differences in Accepting and Receiving Requests for Tasks with Low Promotability," *American Economic Review* 107, no. 3 (January 2017): 14–47, gap.hks.harvard.edu/breaking-glass-ceiling -%E2%80%9Cno%E2%80%9D-gender-differences -declining-requests-non%E2%80%90promotable-tasks.

10. These insights were inspired by the Native Genius® Method taught by Kristen Wheeler.

## Chapter 5: Chasing Gold Standards versus Your True North Star

1. Inspired by Esther and Jerry Hicks, *Ask and It Is Given: Learning to Manifest Your Desires* (Carlsbad, CA: Hay House, 2004), 207–10.

## Chapter 6: From Tunnel Vision to Visionary

1. George Markowsky, "information theory," Brittanica, last modified June 16, 2017, britannica.com/science /information-theory/Physiology.

2. Belle Beth Cooper, "How Naps Affect Your Brain and Why You Should Have One Every Day," Buffer, July 25, 2013, buffer.com/resources/how-naps-affect-your-brain-and -why-you-should-have-one-every-day/; Wayne W. Dyer, "How Do You Sleep?" Wayne's Blog, September 12, 2012, drwaynedyer.com/blog/how-do-you-sleep/.

3. Hal Hershfield, "You Make Better Decisions If You 'See' Your Senior Self," *Harvard Business Review*, June 2013, hbr.org/2013/06/you-make-better-decisions-if-you-see-your -senior-self; Jeremy Bailenson and Laura L. Carstensen, "Connecting to the Future Self: Using Web-Based Virtual

Reality to Increase Retirement Saving," Stanford Health Policy, Freeman Spogli Institute for International Studies, accessed May 2021, healthpolicy.fsi.stanford.edu/research/connecting _to_the_future_self_using_webbased_virtual_reality_to _increase_retirement_saving.

4. Esther and Jerry Hicks, *Ask and It Is Given: Learning to Manifest Your Desires* (Carlsbad, CA: Hay House, 2004), 217–224.

5. Rick Hanson, *Buddha's Brain: The Practical Neuroscience of Happiness, Love, and Wisdom* (Oakland, CA: New Harbinger Publications, 2009).

6. This practice is inspired by Esther and Jerry Hicks, *Ask and It Is Given*, 207–10; as well as Ari Weinzweig, "The Power of Visioning," Zingtrain, accessed May 2021, zingtrain.com /article/the-power-of-visioning/.

## Chapter 7: Radical Responsibility

1. Training materials courtesy of the Hendricks Institute, 2011.

2. Jack Canfield and Janet Switzer, *The Success Principles: How to Get from Where You Are to Where You Want to Be* (New York: HarperCollins, 2005), 6.

3. Credited to Stephen R. Covey, potentially based on the work of psychologist Rollo May.

4. Eleanor A. Maguire, Katherine Woollett, and Hugo J. Spiers, "London Taxi Drivers and Bus Drivers: A Structural MRI and Neuropsychological Analysis," *Hippocampus* 16, no. 12 (December 2006): doi:10.1002/hipo.20233.

5. Training materials courtesy of the Hendricks Institute, 2011.

6. Training materials courtesy of the Hendricks Institute, 2011.

7. Training materials courtesy of the Hendricks Institute, 2011.

8. Adapted from Gay Hendricks, *The Big Leap: Conquer Your Hidden Fear and Take Life to the Next Level* (San Francisco: HarperOne, 2010), 147.

## Chapter 8: Quieting Your Inner Critic

1. Anne Lamott, "My Mind Is a Bad Neighborhood I Try Not to Go Into Alone," Salon, March 13, 1997, salon.com/1997/03/13/lamott970313/.

2. Tara Brach, "The Wisdom of 'It's Not My Fault': Finding Freedom When We Are Caught in Self-Blame," Tara Brach (blog), August 9, 2017, blog.tarabrach.com/2017/08/the -wisdom-of-its-not-my-fault-finding.html.

3. Claire E. Adams and Mark R. Leary, "Promoting Self–Compassionate Attitudes Toward Eating among Restrictive and Guilty Eaters," *Journal of Social and Clinical Psychology* 26, no. 10 (2007): 1120–44, doi: 10.1521/jscp.2007.26.10.1120.

4. Kelly McGonigal, *The Willpower Instinct: How Self-Control Works, Why It Matters, and What You Can Do to Get More of It* (New York: Avery, 2013).

5. Helen Spielman, "Self-Compassion and High Performance Standards: Are They Compatible?" Audition Cafe, August 8, 2017, auditioncafe.com/article/self-compassion-and-high -performance-standards-are-they-compatible/.

6. Kristin D. Neff, "The Science of Self-Compassion," in *Compassion and Wisdom in Psychotherapy*, ed. Christopher K. Germer and Ronald D. Siegel (New York: Guilford Press, 2012), 79–92.

7. Kristin Neff, "Self-Compassion: An Alternative Conceptualization of a Healthy Attitude Toward Oneself," *Self and Identity*, no. 2 (2003): 85–101, doi:10.1080/15298860390129863.

8. Kristin D. Neff and Katie A. Dahm, "Self-Compassion: What It Is, What It Does, and How It Relates to Mindfulness," in

*Handbook of Mindfulness and Self-Regulation*, ed. Brian D. Ostafin, Michael D. Robinson, and Brian P. Meier (New York: Springer, 2015), 121–37.

## Chapter 9: What Limits You?

1. Meeri Kim, "Study Finds That Fear Can Travel Quickly Through Generations of Mice DNA," *Washington Post*, December 7, 2013, washingtonpost.com/national /health-science/study-finds-that-fear-can-travel-quickly -through-generations-of-mice-dna/2013/12/07/94dc97f2 -5e8e-11e3-bc56-c6ca94801fac_story.html.

2. Mark Wolynn, *It Didn't Start with You: How Inherited Family Trauma Shapes Who We Are and How to End the Cycle* (New York: Penguin, 2017), 20.

3. Gay Hendricks, *The Learning to Love Yourself Workbook* (New York: Simon and Schuster, 1990), 8.

## Chapter 10: The Success Myth

1. Arianna Huffington, *Thrive: The Third Metric to Redefining Success and Creating a Life of Well-Being, Wisdom, and Wonder* (New York: Harmony Books, 2015), 1.

2. Gerda Lerner, *The Creation of Patriarchy* (Oxford: Oxford University Press, 1986), 12–13.

3. Lerner, *Creation of Patriarchy*, 228–29.

4. David Kestenbaum, "Keynes Predicted We Would Be Working 15-Hour Weeks: Why Was He So Wrong?" NPR, August 13, 2015, npr.org/2015/08/13/432122637 /keynes-predicted-we-would-be-working-15-hour-weeks-why -was-he-so-wrong.

5. Celeste Headlee, *Do Nothing: How to Break Away from Overworking, Overdoing, and Underliving* (New York: Harmony Books 2020), 43.

6. Kate Manne, *Down Girl: The Logic of Misogyny* (New York: Oxford University Press, 2018), 301.

7. Jen Sincero, *You Are a Badass: How to Stop Doubting Your Greatness and Start Living an Awesome Life* (Philadelphia: Running Press, 2013), 59.

8. Brigid Schulte, *Overwhelmed: Work, Love, and Play When No One Has the Time* (New York: Farrar, Straus and Giroux, 2014), 67.

9. Jonathan B. Spira, *Overload! How Too Much Information is Hazardous to your Organization* (Hoboken, NJ: Wiley, 2011).

10. Jim Sollisch, "Multitasking Makes Us a Little Dumber," *Chicago Tribune*, August 10, 2010, chicagotribune.com /opinion/ct-xpm-2010-08-10-ct-oped-0811-multitask -20100810-story.html; Brigid Schulte, *Overwhelmed: Work, Love, and Play When No One Has the Time* (New York: Farrar, Straus and Giroux, 2014).

11. Headlee, *Do Nothing*, 219–220.

12. Belief Reprogramming created in collaboration with executive coach Sherri Lassila.

## Chapter 11: Permission to Be a Slacker

1. Brigid Schulte, *Overwhelmed: Work, Love, and Play When No One Has the Time* (New York: Farrar, Straus and Giroux, 2014), 68. See also Christena Nippert-Eng, *Home and Work: Negotiating Boundaries Through Everyday Life* (Chicago: University of Chicago Press, 2008); Christena Nippert-Eng, "'Mommy, Mommy' or 'Excuse Me, Ma'am': Gender and Interruptions at Home and Work" (paper presented at the American Sociology Association annual meeting, Pittsburgh, Pennsylvania, August 1992).

2. Arin N. Reeves, *Mansplaining, Manterrupting & Bropropriating: Gender Bias and the Pervasive Interruption of Women*, Nextions, Yellow Paper Series, 2015,

research.umich.edu/wp-content/uploads/2021/12
/manterruptions-bropropriation-and-mansplaining-2-yellow
-paper-series.pdf; Adrienne B. Hancock and Benjamin J.
Rubin, "Influence of Communication Partner's Gender on
Language," *Journal of Language and Social Psychology* 34,
no. 1 (2015): 46–64, jls.sagepub.com/content/34/1/46.full
.pdf+html.

3. Tim Smith-Laing and Fiona Robinson, *An Analysis of Virginia
Woolf's A Room of One's Own* (London: Macat Library, 2017), 96.

## Chapter 12: The Upward Spiral

1. Matthew McConaughey, *Greenlights* (New York: Crown,
2020), 258–61.

2. Mary Oliver, "The Journey," in *Dream Work* (New York:
Atlantic Monthly Press, 1986), 38.

3. This sage advice was given to me by my mentor Carole Robin,
coauthor of *Connect: Building Exceptional Relationships with
Family, Friends, and Colleagues.*

4. Helen Schucman and Bill Thetford, eds., *A Course in Miracles*,
third edition (Mill Valley, CA: Foundation for Inner Peace, 2007).

# ABOUT THE AUTHOR

Vanessa Loder is an inspirational keynote speaker and women's leadership expert whose work has been featured in *Forbes*, *Fast Company*, *Huffington Post*, and *Glamour*, among others. Vanessa received her MBA from Stanford University and her BA from Columbia University, where she graduated Phi Beta Kappa, summa cum laude. Loder is an executive coach certified by the Hendricks Institute, trained in neuro-linguistic programming, past-life regression, and quantum healing hypnosis. Vanessa currently lives in Lafayette, California, with her husband and two children, who remind her to take "mommy time-outs" when she's about to lose her marbles.

Visit her at vanessaloder.com or on Instagram @vanessa.loder.

# ABOUT
# SOUNDS TRUE

Sounds True is a multimedia publisher whose mission is to inspire and support personal transformation and spiritual awakening. Founded in 1985 and located in Boulder, Colorado, we work with many of the leading spiritual teachers, thinkers, healers, and visionary artists of our time. We strive with every title to preserve the essential "living wisdom" of the author or artist. It is our goal to create products that not only provide information to a reader or listener but also embody the quality of a wisdom transmission.

For those seeking genuine transformation, Sounds True is your trusted partner. At SoundsTrue.com you will find a wealth of free resources to support your journey, including exclusive weekly audio interviews, free downloads, interactive learning tools, and other special savings on all our titles.

To learn more, please visit SoundsTrue.com/freegifts or call us toll-free at 800.333.9185.

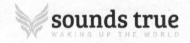

sounds true
WAKING UP THE WORLD